Robbin' The Hood

© D. Jay Thompson

Sea Foam

SEA FOAM PUBLISHING

THE LIBRARY OF CONGRESS HAS CATALOGED

THE SOFT COVER EDITION AS FOLLOWS

Thompson, D. Jay

Robbin' the Hood / D. Jay Thompson

ISBN   9781620302453

10 9 8 7 6 5 4 3 2 1

Professor Padgett Powell
&
The Bar Test

Anabelle, Abraham (bubba), Mandy and Brad

I wish to thank
Fredrick G. Redinger
for his insightful critique and help with this work.

EDITED by Emily Taveras
to whom I am most grateful.

Chapter One

On this night, one of the worse storms in Georgia history passed on its way north. Black clouds covered the skies. In Atlanta you could see the clouds churning to the centrifugal forces of Mother Nature. Sam had just met Rob earlier that evening in a local bar outside the Georgia-Florida border. The bar was nothing more than a cracker shack set up with a sign out front that said "GIRLS, GIRLS, GIRLS!" At nine o'clock the mud was so deep outside that no one was leaving for a while. Sam and Rob hit it off well. They chased a few girls around the pool table and had some beers. It wasn't long before they considered themselves brothers (although that could have been the booze talking).

They finished their last game of pool around three in the morning. "Hey, Rob," said Sam smiling. "I have to go south and I need to catch a train. It was a pleasure meeting you dude."

Sam walked around the corner of the table and stuck his hand out at Rob. Rob was taken back. He wasn't ready to say goodbye to the first friend he had met since leaving home. Rob jumped in quickly, "Now wait just a minute. You can't show up, have fun, and leave. What would the girls say?" The girls began to show pouting faces holding their breasts with both hands and shaking them at Sam.

"I can't help it my friend. I have a schedule to keep." Sam was down to his last dollar. Rob's face crunched up like a squeezed candy wrapper as he said,

"All right then, I'm coming with you." Which surprised the hell out of Sam.

"Dude, you just met me. You don't even know me and now you want to tag along?"

"Look Sam," said Rob. "I know a good thing when I see it. Let's get going so we can catch that train." "Okay dude, but you have no idea what you're getting into." Rob came around the table. They both waved goodbye to the girls and walked out the door.

The boys headed south on Forest Street. Sam was making his way to the train tracks where he firmly believed Rob would end up back at the bar after seeing what Sam had planned. Rob had long legs and had no problem keeping with Sam's pace.

"Hey man. You're walking pretty fast. What time is the train?" Rob asked.

"The tracks are coming up around the corner, you should hear it soon."

"Where are you going to get the tickets?" Rob asked.

"That's just it Rob. We won't need tickets."

The train light came into view about a half mile down the tracks. It was a CSX slow mover coming out of Atlanta. The cars would roll their way down to Miami. The two engines hauled sixty box cars. Sam had a smile on his face. He looked at Rob who was staring down the tracks at the oncoming train. Rob turned to face Sam and said,

"You have got to be kidding me. You're going to ride that thing?"

"You betcha Rob, it's the only free travel left to those with no money," Sam chuckled. He grabbed Rob by the shoulder and pushed him toward a stand of bushes.

"Let's keep behind the bushes until the engine passes. Sometimes the conductor nods off during their ride and we can get on much easier." The engine of the train rumbled up to the boys and passed.

Sam saw the conductor was in fact nodded off. The train moved at about six miles per hour which made it easy for the boys to latch on with their hands and swing themselves aboard. They boarded a yellow freight line car and closed the door. It was dark except for the spear of light that came through a hole in the roof. They sat down with their backs to the wall of the car. Like puppets their bodies jerked to the swaying and bumping of the car on the tracks. Rob reached into his jean jacket pocket and produced a bottle of whiskey three quarters full.

Sam's eyes grew wider, "Where did you get that?" He asked, reaching over to grab the bottle, which Rob pulled it out of reach.

"To slow my friend," a smile breaking on his face. It was a going away present from the girls. Diane slipped it in my pocket during her goodbye kiss." Rob unscrewed the cap and took a long drink then passed the bottle to Sam as the train bumped and nudged them on their way.

The boys traveled for a few hours crossing the border into Florida. They were pretty drunk after a while and talked for a couple hours of old girlfriends and their families. Neither talked much about why they had left home. Sam remembered a place he had stopped at before. It was an old trailer park near the tracks. The train kept up its rickety rackety noise. Sam pointed to the door.

"Rob, we have to get off now." Sam was rocking back and forth trying to get up. Rob looked at Sam and turned on his knees, put his hands on the wall of the car, and barfed. He fell back when he finished. Sam grabbed the shoulder of his jacket and dragged him to the door of the car.

Rob pulled himself to where his head hung out the doorway.

"Sam, you have got to be kidding." Just then, Sam fell out of the car. His grip pulled Rob with him. The boys fell about three feet onto the stones of the sub-grade. They continued rolling down an embankment until it ended near a stand of bushes. Rob's hand fell into one bush scaring a rabbit.

When they stopped moving Sam asked, "Are you okay Rob?" Rob lifted his head and checking all his body parts.

"Never better. Never in my life have I done anything like that Sam" He rolled on his back to stare at the moon. Sam got up and grabbed Rob by the shoulders. Nothing he could do seemed to help Rob stand on his long rubbery legs.

"I know a place where we can sleep," he told Rob. Rob came out of his daze and started walking. They made it across the street to an old abandoned trailer park. They found a mobile home that had a roof at over one room. It was clean given that the roof was missing in most rooms. Sam thought about his mom for a minute and then nodded off. Rob was lying on his back. He thought he was dreaming about school buses, stop signs, and children. He wasn't feeling good at all. He passed into a world of dreams but not before barfing up some stale booze.

The sun poked its way into the morning darkness. Striped awnings were no match for it's light.

The bluish-yellow curtains couldn't keep out the brightness. A blade of sun passed through a side window into a room where a body lay in one corner. A loud snort and fart emitted from the body as its arm dropped to one side.

Sam Gamble snored his way into new day. He was a young man who left home in search of action and living in the fast lane. He was almost six foot high and had an average round face. Sam looked like the kind of young man all the women swooned over. He was a person who could get lost in a crowd. But he was also a hard worker and an intelligent person. He did have problems with authority figures. He didn't do drugs, but once knocked a guy out because he took his parking space. His rap sheet spoke of robberies and petty crimes. All crimes were dismissed due to a lack of evidence.

The sun moved its way to the south end of the home where a rust colored door dropped face down from years of neglect. Hinges taken by the elements. The sun knifed its way in toward another body lying flat on its back. Crumpled cookies and Crackerjack spread out on the floor.

The chest of the body sported a Pink Floyd emblem on a T-Shirt that sparkled in the morning sun. Robert Bertram was a tall young man about six foot three. His pencil-thin figure made his clothes look baggy. He believed that his goal in life was meeting the right people and enjoying what he could before he died. At the moment his body looked dead. Rob slept with his eyes open. His rap sheet showed theft as its main entry and countless misdemeanors.

The town they ended up in was small to say the least. After Sunday church the towns people went out for lunch. Sam was up and standing over Rob, listening to his snore. He couldn't believe Rob slept with his eyes open. It wasn't long before Rob and Sam were hovering around the doorway of an old hardware store. This position gave them the best view of the local restaurant. They watched people come and go for most of the early afternoon.

A well dressed old man and young girl came out and walked toward the parking lot across the street from the restaurant. The man and girl saw the boys. The young girl smiled at Sam and received the same in return.

Rob ran around the building and approached from the back alley. Sam made his way to the car the old man stood next to. Rob came out from behind a Ford Expedition. He moved next to the girl's side of the car and cupped his hand around the girl's mouth. He whispered in her ear, "Say nothing and no one gets hurt."

Sam grabbed the old man in the same manner, bringing his chin up to the side of the old man's face,

"Listen old man," said Sam in a menacing tone. "Give us your wallet and the girl stays healthy." The man, now fearing for the life of his grandchild, reached into his pocket and pulled out his wallet. He held it up in the air where Sam grabbed it. He turned the old man around, keeping his left hand over his mouth.

"Alright, old man," said Sam his voice as rough as gravel. "Now we're going to take the girl to the alley where we will let her go if you haven't made a sound. If you make a sound you will never see her again, do you understand me?" The old man shook his head yes a few times. Sam pushed the old man toward the car door and barked, "Get in the car, close and lock the door and wait for the kid."

The old man followed the instructions. The boys walked behind the parked cars toward the back alley. No one had seen them. Rob put his mouth near the ear of the girl, "Okay kid, you're to go straight to the old man's car. Once you're in the car tell him to count to one hundred. If we hear the car start up or any noise we'll come back and kill you both. Do you understand?" The girl nodded her head in affirmation. Rob removed his hand from her mouth and pushed her forward, "Now get! And don't forget what I said."

Rob and Sam turned and ran down the alley. They mapped out a plan that provided for even the most unexpected situation that could occur. They stopped and listened, but heard nothing. The old man must be still counting. They split up. Rob ran through a yard that led to a forest while Sam ran farther down the road to a field where corn grew six feet high.

Sam slowed to a fast walk and pushing the stalks out of his way entered the field moving toward to its center. He knew Rob would be along in a minute. He heard thrashing coming from not too far away and then Rob spoke.

"Sam? Where the hell are you?"

Sam came from Rob's right side pushing away the corn stalks. "Will you shut up? Do you want everyone to know where we are? We need to get out of here." Sam opened the wallet and found two credit cards and seventeen dollars in cash. He gave Rob the seven dollar bills and stuffed the ten in his pocket. Sam dug up about a foot of loose dirt with his shoe and threw the wallet in after wiping it down with his T-shirt. He then buried it. Rob looked at Sam and asked,

"What's next?" Sam was still upset from Rob yelling. His eyes burned with anger, but then softened.

"There's a train that comes through here at about three thirty," said Sam. "It'll be going south. We best get on it. Let's blow this corn patch and get to the tracks." He turned and started to walk out of the last row of sweet corn. He turned back and grabbed an ear for a snack. Rob followed suit, grabbing two and jammed one in his back pocket.

There was a commotion in front of the restaurant. The girl and the old man were giving descriptions to the police. Sam and Rob were only a field away. They headed for the tracks. Their plan seemed to be working rather well so far. The town Sheriff only had two trooper cars and a nearby college town, had perhaps ten more. What should have been a search and chase ended up going in the wrong direction.

The only way out of town was highway four forty one. There were a few cars directed towards the fields, but the boys were out of there by then. The cops even posted traffic stops at each end of the city, but the boy's were up along the tracks ready for the train. They could see the train approaching in the distance. The troopers didn't expect them to use a train for their escape. They sat on the tracks laughing at the cops.

"We didn't get shit from the old man," said Rob.

"Nah, but we didn't have to fight for it either," said Sam with a positive look on his face. "I have an uncle down in Tampa. We ought to be there in about two hours. He has a room we could stay in for a day or so and food enough for a day after we leave. He won't put us up for more than that though. Some bad blood from the old days with my dad still lingers in his head. He's always been pissed because I didn't finish school. He promised my dad before he died he would get me to finish."

The train was on time. The engine pulled fifty boxcars, all different styles and colors. Sam put stones on the left side of the track. The train hit them and force the conductor would pay attention to that side of the train. Just as the stones shot out from under the wheels of the slow moving train, the boy's shot out from a large grassy bush and ran to an open door in a box car. Sam grabbed the boarding grip on the side and putting a foot

in the car rolled inside. He then reached down to help
Rob get in. They both lay on the bed of the boxcar
catching their breath when they heard muffled laughing
coming from one of the corners.

Both Sam and Rob bolted into a standing
position but couldn't see anything. The car had a panel
halfway through its center. Their eyes had not adjusted
to the darkness yet. It took a moment for their eyes to
adjust when they peered around the panel. They saw a
hat with two eyes under it staring back.

A man began to stand and brush off the sleeves of
his overcoat. He was tall and lanky. His clothes ill fitting
the skin and bones beneath. He took a step toward the
boys. The man towered over Rob's six foot four height.
He put one hand around the panel end to stabilize
himself as the car shook going through a turn. His hand
was nothing but bones. His skeletal fingers were
manicured with dirt and cigarette stains. The word C R
O W tattooed across his knuckles gave him the presence
of a man who could handle himself.

The man walked out from the panel, backing up
the boys as he went until they were in the middle of the
boxcar. He took off his hat and said,

"Hello boys. It's been a while since I had
company on a trip. My name is Malcolm Peters." He
smiled and gave a wink. At that point he produced his
other hand to shake. Rob was scared but Sam's face was
hard. He wasn't going to let somebody throw them off
their means of transportation if that was what this guy
had in mind. Sam grabbed the hand and squeezed as
hard as hc could.

"Whoa there my friend, that's a might powerful
grip you've got," Malcolm said. "I'll bet you're a boxer or
wrestler or something." Sam eased off on the grip and
smiled.

"Look boys, I'm not going to try and throw you

off the train, though lord knows there are plenty who would. It'll be great to have some company before I leave. Where you both headed?" He asked with a questioning look in his eyes.

"We're going to Tampa," Rob said.

"Tampa?" Malcolm said. "A lot of nice things going on in Tampa, why, I remember when I first went there back about ten years ago. There was a Hobo City complete with fifty gallon drums burning bright in the winter night. The weather is nice there in the summer too. They had just built a train bridge down near the airport that ran across the bay. Everyone gathered together. What a view. Some singing, some just getting their hands warm, some sleeping off the effects of Hobo Punch after a long trip. Many came from as far as New York. I came down from St. Louis at that time."

"What's Hobo Punch?" Rob asked.

"Hobo Punch?" Malcolm said a bit startled. "Well, it's a concoction the old bums made years ago. Everyone would contribute whatever drink they had, beer, wine, liquor, and they would add some water and bring it to a boil. Then, they would take a piece of leather from a worn out shoe and put it in the pot. They say the leather boiling in the pot absorbed anything that was bad in it. They boiled it for about ten minutes. Then they let it cool and passed it around to all present. They gave up a toast to old number seven."

The boys had not heard a story quite like that before.

"Why old number seven?" Rob asked. Malcolm sat down with his back to the wall. The boys sat too. They crossed their legs as they backed up against the center panel. Malcolm continued tipping his hat farther up his forehead so they could see his full face.

"Well, two reasons actually. The first is that some of the hobos from over a hundred years ago were riding in a boxcar, going through Tennessee, and stopped near Lynchburg. Well, it was the dead of winter so the boys got off because you know the engineer had to check every car. They found a clearing about a quarter mile from the train and lit up a small fire.

A stranger came upon them from the direction of the city. He scared the hell out of them, actually. He had on clean clothes and a tie, tucked into the top of his farmer jeans, and bottles banging around in his pockets. Naturally the men were a little curious. They wondered what was up with all those bottles clinking around in his pockets. He came over to them and said,

'Howdy men, I have something I want you to taste." So he sat down on an old log and when the men saw the clear bottles, full of what looked like moonshine, every tin cup was out and raised. They asked him what his name was.

"Can you guess who it was?" Malcolm's eye-brows shot to the top of his head.

"Who was it?" Rob asked. Malcolm continued,

"It was old Jack Denials. He had been mixing up all kinds of brews and he told the men that this was the sixth batch and he wanted them to try it. Well, when the men took a drink, they spit it out right then and there. Jack was beside himself. He just couldn't figure out what he had done wrong.

"Then, one of the men said to him that they could fix it if he wished. Well, Jack's eyes lit up and he said, 'sure give it your best.' They poured two of the bottles in a pot and boiled it. One of them had some leather to boil. He said it came from a real Indian moccasin. When the water was boiling well over their makeshift fire one the men threw the piece of leather in. It boiled for about five minutes. Then they took it off the heat and let it set.

After it cooled, they poured some into a tin and handed it to Jack. He drank it and could not believe it.

The taste of shine was there but it had taken on a smoother characteristic. He started laughing until his side was going to burst and his jaw hurt. Jack went and shook every ones hand, declaring that Old Number Seven would live on forever. Most people don't know where or how Jack Denials got his recipe for Old Number Seven. We hobos know why it says that on every bottle and we mix it up whenever we have a get together."

Malcolm didn't mention that the taste differed depending on what you were mixing together.

"That's some story," said Sam folding his arms across his chest. Rob's jaw was still open once he figured out who Jack was. Then Malcolm said,

"But, that's not all. The second reason is one of the boys named Whiskers took a liking to old Jack. He ended up following him back to Lynchburg. They arrived the next day in the late morning. Whiskers was surprised to see that Jack and his family had a whiskey still. Jack offered a job to old Whiskers pumping spring water for his still and doing odd jobs around the complex. Whiskers took the job and went to work for Jack. Whiskers died seven years later. Now when we toast, we remember old Whiskers." Malcolm held up his hand high toasting.

"It just gets better all the time," said Sam. Malcolm replied,

"Well, if you don't believe me you can ask any hobo, anywhere, at any time. This story has been handed down from mouth to ear for a hundred years." Then Malcolm turned around and picked up his shoulder bag. The sturdy elm branch it was tied to scraping along the wooden floor of the car. He tossed it out the sliding door of the boxcar and followed right after. He landed with a short slide on the gravel. He waved to the boys and said,

"Carry yourselves well in Tampa and may good fortune come your way." Malcolm quickly disappeared into the brush and bushes alongside the track. It was starting to get dark now. Rob and Sam looked at each other. Sam raised an eyebrow saying,

"At least he left us the pot and some kindling." Rob stuck his head out the side of the boxcar looking back to where he last saw Malcolm,

"Do you think the stones tore up his bare feet any?" Sam looked at Rob, stuck his own head out the doorway looking back, and pulled it in a second later.

"Nope, that dude was about as crusty as a rail bum can get. I felt the calloused fingers and palms of his hand. He lives a hard life. He could have fallen into a brick wall and laughed about it." Rob shook his head.

"Yes. He did look like a grungy homeless person and yet he may have been better off than some I have seen." The boys returned to the kindling to heat up their corn for dinner. Fortunately there was little smoke from the fire. The boys bit into their corn and found it juicy. After eating they laid back against the car side and listening to the sounds of the trains wheels moving on the track and the slight swaying of the car the boys rested from the day.

Chapter Two

The train pulled into the hub near Tampa and the boys made their jump when it slowed almost to a stop. They had to cut across three other tracks before finding the relative security of a large bush. They could be arrested for trespassing if they were caught. Sam wasn't too happy. What were once large scraggy bushes and small trees had then changed to manicured lawns and palms. It could have been part of some beautification program down here over the years.

The boys walked under two raised expressway ramps just to get to his uncle's neighborhood. The hood was filled with low-rent style homes and cracker shacks. Small one bedroom houses occupied the first block. Many of the houses provided living quarters for as many as six to eight people. Most hung out on the front porch, especially if new people were walking down the street, whole families seemed to unfold in front of them.

Uncle Felix was Sam's father's brother. He ran drugs for the cartels for many years. Today he works for the Colombian cartel bringing cocaine up from Miami. The blow travels up from Miami to Tampa. Then it heads through Illinois and makes many stops along the way.

Felix's house was not pretentious and blended in well with the neighbors. The inside was another story. Opulent furniture lay throughout the living areas. A large Victorian picture covered six twenty-four inch television screens used for surveillance. The screens picked up the boys on their way to the house.

Uncle Felix liked Sam. He knew he needed some fathering. It just wasn't his style. He still felt responsible for getting his brother killed though. Felix lived in the fast lane and made much use of his cartel allowance. He opened the door just as the boys topped the last step.

"Sam, Sam, Sam," Felix said with a smile across his face. How long has it been?" He stepped forward and gave Sam a big hug. "I seriously remember you being much shorter. You look weathered and in need of some food. Who do we have here?" Felix asked, walking toward Rob and putting a hand on his shoulder.

"This is my friend Rob," Sam replied.

"Well, nice to meet you Rob, come on in boys we'll get you some food and drink. You want to shower, it's down the hall on your left, there are towels in the closet," said Felix. Sam jumped in,

"I remember Uncle. It's only been a year since I was here and the place hasn't changed a bit." Sam looked around the room. He noticed a change in the pictures.

"I could use a shower," said Rob looking at Sam. Sam quickly cuffed him on the back of the head. They both began to walk down the hall. Rob didn't do anything unless it was okay with Sam. It wasn't as if Sam was controlling Rob but it came close. Rob wasn't stupid by any means either, it was just the way Sam rolled, and

Rob was becoming aware. Rob liked Sam though he felt he could be a dangerous type of guy, if the circumstances required it.

The boys showered and met with Sam's uncle in the kitchen. Felix had a maid who did all the cooking and cleaning. She also sold crack to the teens down at the bowling alley on the weekends.

The boys sat down at a boat table meant for an executive office. The table was called this due to the fact it was shaped like the bottom of a John boat. It had inlaid mother of pearl triangles surrounding the outer edges in a one-up, one-down pattern, and the center was an inlaid mosaic of a unicorn, its wings spreading the full length of the table. The chairs were high-backed solid spruce. The seats were like velvet of some kind and felt more like the pictures of Elvis sold on Beal Street. The kitchen on the whole was small and the table took up most of the room. The appliances were stainless steel. Felix even had a Jen-Air installed for the nice thick steaks he was so fond of. As the boys pulled out chairs for themselves, three girls came in the room chewing gum, flipping their hair, and acting like teens, posed with that knee bent, drop hip, hand on waist stance. The first one was the tallest of the bunch and as her eyes grew large said,

"Hey Sammy, long time no talk huh? What you been up too?"

Her smile was a mile wide across her face. She showed a beautiful set of teeth any dentist would marvel at and her complexion was like burnt umber. She wore a T-shirt with the words "Sex Pistols" stenciled across it. She also wore a blue jean vest, tight shorts, and socks that came up to her knees. She had patent leather boots that looked like she wore mirrors on her feet. She had blond hair cropped close like a tomboy. Her face had a bunch of freckles on the upper part of each cheek that spread out like the measles when she smiled.

Sam's eyes grew wild at seeing the girl.

"Hey Tabitha, man, you have grown some. I thought you'd be in school until at least three this afternoon. It's good to see you. Who are these other fine looking girls?" The other girls smiled and gave Sam a sort of curtsy. The red head spoke first,

"Hi Sammy, my name is Loretta, I live next door and I'm Tabby's BFF."

A black haired girl, blond roots showing on her scalp, turned her head toward Sam and said,

"Hey Sammy, you remember me don't you? In the tool shed out back in my yard. You better remember you weasel." Sam pushed his chair back at the threat responding to the menacing voice,

"Hi Marcie, yes I remember, man, you have grown up as well as out. It's nice to see you again. Before he could move, Marcie picked a towel up from the table and threw it at his face. His hand came up quickly and caught it. He got up and ran toward the girls who scattered squealing. Just before Marcie got through the door Sam wound up the towel and snapped it across her ass. You could hear the crack downstairs. Just then, Sam's uncle Felix walked back into the room, his eyes wide with concern.

"Now hold on, young man. This is no place for a free-for-all towel spanking session. This is a kitchen. I want you all to behave yourselves. Girls, Sam and his friend Rob are going to be staying with us for a day or so. I want you to be on your best behavior and that means no roughhousing, especially in the kitchen. I'm sorry, Miss Nana," Felix said in apology to the older women who walked in from the pantry. "Now Tabitha, you're my daughter and Sam's cousin. I expect you to take care of him while I go downtown to do some business. I'll be home at nine. Remember there's a party for some people from down south tonight. I expect this place to be spotless when I get back."   Tabitha grabbed the door jamb and swung her head around it.

"Okay, daddy. I'll take care of Sammy and his friend and we will pick up the place so Nana has less work to do. Sammy, you and Rob get something to eat. I assume that was why you were in the kitchen instead of downstairs. We'll meet up in about half an hour when we're done cleaning. See ya!" Sam stuck his hand up and waved.

"Okay see you soon then Tabby."
Nana leaned against the stove. She watched what was unfolding in her kitchen as if it had happened every day since she began to cook for Felix. She walked over to the boys and asked what they wanted to eat. Both agreed on some eggs, sunny side up, hash browns and bacon. Nana started for the stove and saw the silver dove necklace hanging on Sam's neck. She stopped in her tracks and smacked Sam on the head.

"Is that my silver dove?" Nana asked. Sam, forgetting how he came by it, flew off the chair and out of the room. Nana was close behind yelling,

"When I get my hands on you I'm gonna pull all the hair out your head, you little thieving bastard." Sam took off in the direction of the front door and barely made it before Nana's fingers just missed his shirt.

He pounded down the front stairs and hit the sidewalk running full blast. His ears burned from all the cuss words Nana was yelling from the porch. Sam knew he was going to miss lunch and maybe dinner too. He reached the end of the block and started walking toward the corner store. He figured he would fill up on a few snowballs and soda using the money from the old man.

Rob sat amused at Sam's actions and a half laugh came out of his mouth just as Nana starting chasing Sam out of the room. He did bend his head around the doorway and was laughing more when Nana almost caught Sam at the top of the stairs. *Man that lady could move* Rob thought.

Nana came back through the door and Rob quickly went and sat down again. She returned to the kitchen red in the face and huffing.

"Damn, I'm getting to old for this. Okay boy, you just give me a few minutes and I am going to make you the best breakfast you ever had." Rob thanked her in advance and waited. The last piece of sausage left Rob's fork. He was about as full as you can get without bursting. He thanked Nana again for the breakfast just as the girls came through the door.

"Hey, where's Sammy?" They all asked at once.

"Did he have a problem with your cooking, Nana?" Marcie asked with a menacing look on her face. The last time she got with Sammy things were a lot different.

"Well, he was running," Said Rob, "but not from the food." He glanced over at Nana who winked at the girls. "Anyway, I'm not sure where he is or if he will be back anytime soon," he said with a smile on his face.

"Well then," said Tabitha, "You're all ours." C'mon let's go downstairs. We have a few hours before the party. You can watch us girls work on the play we are doing for school." She skipped toward the stairwell where the other girls were waiting. Rob thanked Nana and began to follow the girls downstairs.

The stairs were wider than most basement staircases. The left side wall showed a picture every few feet. They showed Sam's uncle with military people dressed in Iraqi military uniforms. There were stacks of bombs and missiles standing up against crates in most of the pictures. Each one had him shaking hands with a different dignitary.

Rob thought Sam's uncle might have been an arms dealer at one time. This didn't sit well with Rob as his father passed away due to an arms dealer. The man ratted him out while on a U.S. military mission when he was in the military special forces. Sam said he was a drug dealer now.

Rob reached the end of the stairs and walked into what he thought was a party during the seventies. Streamers ran from almost every point of the room's ceiling. Fine nets like those used for mosquitoes had been draped in all the corners and stuffed with balloons. There were speakers the likes of which Rob had only seen at concerts. In fact, there was a stage with a set of drums and keyboards at the far end.

The basement was long. He thought it might be longer than the house actually was. If this was true, it had to have been built under the back yard. Rob was more than a little curious. Still, he was a guest here and because of this he wouldn't ask any questions. The girls were over on the right side behind a curtain. He could tell this because that location was where the giggles were coming from.

Rob grabbed the top of a psychedelic colored cloth that fronted the area and moved it open enough to sneak a peek. All three of the girls had the most elaborate southern princess dresses on. One of the girls was tying bows in their hair. When he peeked in-between the folds he saw they were trying to zip up their zippers. Tabitha had not seen Rob move the curtain.

"We'll just be a minute Rob. Would you go over and turn on the iPod? It's at the end of the room on the old dresser. Thanks,"

Another giggle came out of the girls. They were having fun. Rob turned and looked down to the end of the room, saw the iPod, and started walking toward it. He noticed a large Chinese painting on the wall to his left. It depicted Samurai warriors on horses throwing spears at a tiger. A few spears were already in the tiger's back. The tiger had exaggerated claws that looked like sharp needles.

Rob turned on the iPod and the song 'Party like its 1999' by Prince started a bit loud from the speakers in the room. Rob saw a chair next to the dresser and sat down. It appeared he was in for a show.

The girls came out of the curtain dancing and lip syncing the words to the song. Each one took their turn with a line. Rob wasn't sure what he was watching since the dresses did not match the song's era in time. The girls looked like thirteenth century medieval maidens singing rock & roll. Their acting brought a smile to Rob's face.

He looked them over with his eyes settling on Tabitha, who among the three, actually looked beautiful in what she was wearing. He couldn't take his eyes off her. Her arm movements were like the wings of a butterfly and she moved with a grace he had not seen in any girl before. It was as if she were born to be a dancer. All three glided in unison. Rob thought they had their moves down enough to pull off whatever it was they were doing. A phone rang. You could barely hear it over the music and the girls did not appear to notice. Rob reached up and turned down the volume of the iPod. The girls stopped.

"That's my phone," Marcie said, and rushed to where the girls were first changing. Everyone waited until she put the phone to her ear.

"Hello? What! He fell off what? I'll be right there," With a look of horror on her face, "Guys I have to go. My dad fell off the roof trying to install a dish and he's hurt pretty bad. I know I said I would help you Tabby." Tabitha's face showed deep worry.

"No way Marcie, just go take care of your dad and

don't worry about this place. Then Loretta said,

"Tab, I'm going with Marcie. It's just the two of them living together and I might be able to help them. We'll see you later for the party okay?" Tabitha shooed them into the curtained area.

"That's fine, but you have five blocks to run and you won't make it in those outfits. Now get them off and get going."

Rob sat there wondering if her father would be okay. He also wondered what Sam was doing and why he didn't come back. The thought of Sam actually being afraid of Nana seemed surreal. She seemed like a nice lady if you didn't piss her off.

Marci and Loretta ran up the stairs after changing and Tabitha began to clean the basement. Rob saw a bottle of furniture cleaner and a cloth sitting on a table. He started to spray and dust the cabinets. He was being extra careful to wipe all of the parts. He moved next to the book shelves and began to dust the edges. He noticed the books were pretty old and a few looked like they were falling apart. One of the books was titled 'God's Work'. He grabbed it, but only the top came toward him.

At the same time a click was heard near a panel. It slipped open a couple inches. He opened the door a bit more and stuck his head inside. It looked like another basement ran between the house Rob was in and the one next door. There must have been ten people working down there. They were packing white powder into plastic bags. Then he heard Tabitha come up from behind,

"Oh my God, what on earth made you pull that book? You were not supposed to know about this. My dad will kill me," she said with a scared look on her face.

"Tabitha, no one saw me," a smile appearing on his face.

"Hurry up, close it and put the book back. I won't say anything to my dad. He would have you killed. Especially since you're only a friend of Sammy's and not real family. You're lucky I like you Rob," she said with a stern face that turned into a sexy little smile.

Their faces were alarmingly close together. She closed her eyes and moved to kiss him. He let her. His arms enfolded her slim tight body. She put her arms around his neck and they fell on a nearby leather futon. Her skin was as soft as her hair. In between kisses he would look into her eyes of ocean blue so clear he could almost see her soul.

Rob had made love once before but it was a long time ago. Her hand massage caused him to bulge. He began to move his lips down her neck and chewed lightly on her earlobes. His hands surrounded her young breasts and found hard nipples waiting. Just then Nana was coming down the stairs. They broke up and tried to control their breathing just as she came in sight. Rob had grabbed the furniture polish again and was working on the rails of the futon.

Tabitha was walked toward Nana. Nana looked around the room.

"Well now, you managed to put the boy to work. There is something about us women folk that make men either scatter or take to cleaning like they were born to it. I appreciate you both cleaning up down here." Rob now gave her his full attention.

"Sure thing Nana," he said with a smile on his face. "it's the least I could do after having such a great breakfast, I'm still full from it."

"Okay then," Nana said. "It looks like this place is ready for the party. I need to start making food for tonight. We are going to have smoked ham with all the fixings." Nana turned and walked back up the stairs. Tabitha was unable to wait and ran over to Rob.

She threw her arms around his neck giving him a big kiss.

"I have to go change. I also need to call Marcie to see how her father is doing. Go upstairs and ask to help Nana. If you get on her good side, nobody will hurt you around here." Tabitha went into the curtained area and Rob went up the stairs. She rumbled up the stairs not long after. Rob was walking toward the kitchen. Just as he passed the dining room, a hand came out and covered his mouth, it smelled like candy and coconuts. He was pulled into the bath. It was Sam. His eyes were darting this way and that looking for Nana.

"Look Rob I'm in a jam. I took this necklace last time I was here but I didn't know it belonged to Nana. You have to help me out of this," pleaded Sam. Rob stood there staring at him for a moment.

"What can I do?" Rob said. Rob wasn't a big thinker when it came to getting out of trouble. It was one of the reasons the boys worked well together. Sam had the brains that Rob looked to for guidance.

"I'm going to give you the necklace and I want you to give it to Nana and explain that I didn't know it was hers. If I go in there now she will kill me first and ask questions later."

"Okay Sam, I'll go." Rob started walking with the necklace through the dining room and into the kitchen. After a few minutes Sam heard them both laughing. They were almost hysterical. Sam walked into the kitchen making sure the large table and Rob were in between him and Nana. Then he asked,

"What's all the laughing about?"

"You fool," Nana said in between chuckles. "that necklace is no more mine than the house I live in. I was just seeing how fast you could run. And boy did you run like the wind." Sam sat down in the closest chair. Rob thought, after giving Sam a good looking over, that steam might have been building up to come out his ears. Rob told him so and both he and Nana broke out laughing again. Nana banged a pot on the counter. Rob slapped his knee and the table at the same time.

"Fine, fine, fine," he said with a face like stone. "you had some fun at my expense. It caused me to miss a meal. I had to go eat Snowballs from the corner store." Both Rob and Nana repeated, "Snowballs," at the same time and burst out laughing all over again. Rob had his head on the table now still laughing. Nana had moved to a chair. She leaned it back.

"Sammy boy," she said with a serious look on her face. "you best get a hold of yourself. Don't let things like this bother you or you're going to grow old real fast," said Nana. She looked Sam straight in the eye, nodded her head, and went back to giggling like a school girl. She noticed Rob had not stopped laughing yet. Sam backhanded Rob's head a little which took the laugh out of him. He still had a smile on his face though. Nana waved them both out of the kitchen. She had a lot to cook yet and it was getting close to time for the party.

Felix was actually out putting a coke deal together with one of the local gangs. His people had been making it in that secret basement. The deal went well for both parties money-wise. There was an extra item that the gang wanted Felix to take care of for them. It seemed one of their members split the gang and took off with a large amount of cash and dope. They thought he went to Chicago and was staying in an apartment near a bowling alley. They hired a private detective to locate the guy but wanted Felix to send someone to take care of him.

To keep things smooth, Felix agreed even though it was not his style. This gang money coming in would be his ticket to the Greek Isles for the rest of his life. Felix would think of something. He came in the house just as the boys were leaving the kitchen. Felix held up a hand.

"Well, there you are. How was your day so far? Has anything happened while I was gone?" He looked from one to the other. Then Sam spoke up,

"Sure uncle, I was chased out of the house for something I didn't do. I missed a meal and then had to listen to Rob and Nana go crazy with laughter because of it."

"Well, I had a great breakfast," said Rob rubbing his hand over his belly. "Then I went downstairs and watched the girls dance for a school project they were working on. Marcie's dad had fallen off his roof. Two of the girls left to help him and I helped to clean up the basement with Tabitha for the party."

"Well I'll be. Whose idea was it to get you to clean the house Rob? You're a guest here. You shouldn't be cleaning anything," Felix stated. Rob had a smile on his face.

"It was my idea and I didn't mind. Tabitha may not have finished by herself so I just helped a bit."

Nodding his head in satisfaction Felix said,

"Well, I sure do appreciate it Rob. Listen boys, about this party. I have a problem that I want Sam to take care of for me. If you have the guts, that is. It's worth a lot of cash to you. The only problem is you'll have to miss the party and leave tonight." The boys looked at each other. Sam turned back to his uncle and said,

"Sure uncle I'll take care of whatever it is you want done." Rob nodded his head yes.

"That's great, boys. Now here is what I need to get done."

They sat down in the living room while Felix explained what had to get done. The boys were a bit startled when Felix mentioned the word kill. Neither of the two had ever killed someone before.

Felix went to the cabinet and took out two automatic nine millimeter guns with silencers. He showed them how they worked and even fired a shot through the ceiling which no one heard in the house. He gave them some cash and told them they could have the car in the garage for the trip. The last thing Felix said was that to make it a legitimate trip, he would be sending Tabitha with them.

He instructed them to take her to her uncle's place and drop her off before they went looking for the guy. He said they could keep half of whatever money the guy had and to bring the cocaine back so he could return it to the gang. The estimated stolen cash was sixty thousand dollars. The boys' eyes lit up upon hearing that number. Of course, they had no idea what the guy had spent. He was only gone from the gang for about two weeks. Sam wondered how much could one spend in three weeks. Then again, Sam could think of a lot of things he could buy that would eat up sixty thousand dollars. Sam had always wanted to be well off. It seemed to him that every time he was getting ahead, something would come along, spoil his dream and reek havoc in his life. He made a pact with himself. If he did get the chance to pocket some real cash, he would make sure that it would be around when he needed it.

Sam began to day dream a bit. He thought about boats, women, motorcycles and fast, awesome cars. The kind of cars you get detailed once a week. He thought about fancy restaurants, large tips and not having to make reservations. Then he thought about Rob. They had not been together all that long. Rob wasn't the sharpest tool in the shed, but then Sam thought, he himself wasn't a genius either.

Sam knew more about street life then Rob did. Rob was just running away from a doting family that smothered him with love he remembered Rob saying. He would make sure to take care of Rob even if it meant his life. Rob was now his best friend. He blew out of his daydream when Rob put his hand on his shoulder shaking him,

"Hey Sam! You in there?" Rob yelled. "We're talking to you." Sam just shrugged his shoulders and walked into the front hall. They said their goodbyes to Nana and Felix and with Tabitha in tow went out to the garage. When they got there their jaws dropped. Inside was a Mercedes three eighty sedan in perfect shape. Sam got in and started her up. The car purred and the chocolate brown color with light brown leather seats matched the jacket Sam wore.

Sam moved the car out of the garage and pressed the door closer. He punched the gas and the car zoomed down the street.

Chapter Three

The boys and girl hit the road heavy, but not heavy enough to persuade a cop to stop them for speeding. They were packing some heat in the car after all. They hit Atlanta around four in the morning and stopped to get a room and some sleep. They rented two rooms actually. It was Tabitha's suggestion. The boys didn't care. Felix gave them plenty of spending cash. They all discussed which would be the best way to travel on a table in the boy's room. Then they all went to sleep.

Rob couldn't sleep. He laid there thinking about the day's events. He felt things were happening fast. He went through the day in his mind until he got to the point where Tabitha kissed him. He had been bitten by the love bug. She was so beautiful. He couldn't get her out of his mind and Sam's snoring wasn't helping matters for thinking. He threw the covers off the bed and slid to the floor. He tucked the key in his pajamas and left the room. He knocked at Tabitha's door. He heard the rustling of covers and movement in the room. Shortly she opened the door.

"Rob, I knew you would come." She grabbed his arm and pulled him into the room. Then she pushed him down on the bed and all this time he was trying to talk.

"Tabitha. I'm sorry, but I just can't stop thinking about you. You're the most beautiful girl I ever met." That was all he could get out of his mouth. In a minute they both had their pajamas off and were lying on the bed. Rob reached behind her and caressed her ass and legs with his long nimble fingers while they kissed. He wasn't a great lover or so he thought. He felt inexperienced.

Tabitha reached down and played with Rob's ample member. He decided to let things play out whatever way they did at this point. She pressed her small round breasts against his chest while they made out. She ran her hands along his chest which, she thought, had just the right amount hair on it. He was kind of skinny, but he did sport a bit of a belly. Nobody was perfect.

Moving with care, he mounted her. She picked up the rhythm and they both began to move faster. He was fondling her breasts when he thought he would explode. He put his arms around her legs and lifted her knees to her ears. Grabbing her shoulders he put all his effort into the finish. She exploded just before he did. A short moan left her lips. Sweat poured down his forehead and cheeks and dripped onto her nose. Exhausted, he dropped to the side of the bed, breathing heavy.

Rob laid there for a while holding Tabitha. Her breathing was heavy also. Neither said a word. Finally Rob said,

"I have to go before Sam finds out I am gone. We don't want any trouble on this trip. I love you." He put his pajamas back on and went out the door with Tabitha saying she loved him too as he was closing it. He went back to his room and opened the door.

Sam turned in his bed.

"Where did you go?"He asked quietly.

"I needed some fresh air. Your snoring was driving me batty," Rob responded. Sam turned back over and went to sleep. Rob stayed up a bit longer thinking about Tabitha. He had feelings for her for sure.

The next morning Sam caught Tabitha staring, not looking, at Rob. Sam knew it was a fifteen hour drive to Chicago and he wanted to get this job done as fast as possible. He also had a desire to get back to some familiar territory. He didn't like being in places he had never been before. Ron and Sam switched off driving. Out of caution they watched the speed limit and slowly made their way north.

They finally made it to the city and dropped Tabitha off at her uncle's house. They said their goodbyes and told Tabitha they would pick her up when they finished the job. The boys traveled down the Kennedy expressway to Western Avenue. Then they followed Western Avenue down to Irving Park Road.

There was a gas station on the corner next to a three story building and a factory across the alley behind the station. Sam had called ahead to set up the meeting with the private investigator. There was a tunnel that ran below the three story building from front to back. They were to meet the private investigator at the stairs on the back side. U-Haul trailers filled the back of the station.

It was late in the evening and the station had closed. Any children that might live in the building would be sound asleep. Sam and Rob walked through the trailers in the back of the station toward the building. The boys were careful not to trip on the trailer tongues sticking out. They made their way over a guard rail and down the stairs into a tunnel. A light was shining on the other end.

The PI asked,

"Is that you Sam? He shined a flashlight down the tunnel. His head looking to either side of the beam.

"Yes, it's me and this is Rob. The PI shifted his position and came down the stairs to meet them in the tunnel. He was bigger than Sam first thought and he seemed to expand as he walked. His body seemed to fill the whole center of the tunnel. He was bald and had tattoos covered most of the exposed areas on his body.

The PI produced a piece of paper.

"This is the address. I am not sure if he is in the basement or the upstairs room but he is, in the house and what's more, he is there right now. I have a guy who works for me keeping an eye on him. He never goes in the back, always the front and we can't tell where after that." The PI's leg shook like he was having a tremor or something. Sam wondered if that was why he wasn't a cop anymore.

"That's all we need to know," said Sam. "We appreciate the help." Sam's raised his hand to shake the PI's.

"Not at all, you're paying for it," the PI said. Then he turned and made his way up the stairs. He turned to the right and walked down to the alley. The boys left the way they came.

The guy they were after held up in one of the bungalow type houses Chicago has sprinkled throughout its urban area. It happened to be next to a bowling alley. The upstairs apartment had only one window and a screened-in porch at the back. The back had a standard yard and garage. Most neighborhoods in Chicago had alleys so the boys thought that to be the best approach.

Sam had picked locks before and was pretty good at it. Neither of the boys were violent people. Sam loved a good fight. It was the reason he stepped forward when the hobo on the train appeared. It was dark now. The moon was just a sliver in the sky. The boys had crouched down behind the garbage cans near the alley of the house. The light was on upstairs and they could see movement through the curtains in the kitchen window. The outline was hard to read but Sam figured it was the guy they were looking for.

Sam put his arm on Rob's shoulder and whispered

"Look Rob, there is no need for you to get into major trouble here. Let's set the safety on your gun so you don't pull the trigger and kill someone, namely me. We don't know who is in the house but the back stairs go to the porch on the second floor. It's one of those older doors we can get into with a credit card. Now look, let me do all the talking when we get inside and let me do the job. Felix is my uncle and we are here because of him. Just follow my lead and point your gun at anyone else who may be with this guy." Sam hoped Rob would do as he planned. Rob seemed not to mind having Sam in control. Rob said, "Okay Sam."

They crept up the narrow sidewalk towards the rear of the house. Sam wondered if this guy had any hidden warning devices around. They took the steps one by one as quiet as they could. Sam's hand brushed against something on the third stair from the top. It was clear filament, the type used for fishing line. It ran about two inches above the edge of the step from side to side. Sam followed the line where it led into the house with his eyes.

"There must be bells or cans attached to the other end," he said to Rob in a whisper. "Make sure you don't step on this line." Rob understood. Sam made it to the top stair and gave the door a good looking over. He checked the side and kitchen window. He decided no one could see the top of the stairs from this position. He happened to bring a little vial of oil with him that he would put on the door hinges to quiet them up.

Rob wondered how Sam could have anticipated the need for oil or if was he just a prepared boy scout. Old doors do squeak. He slipped a credit card he found the other day in the old man's wallet into the lock. He opened the door about an inch and put some silicone drops on the hinge bolts. The door would not open any further. Sam noticed a hook on the door. He lifted up the hook with a pen he had in his pocket. The door swung open.

Sam turned and whispered,

"Okay Rob be careful where you put your feet. Any noise and this guy could bolt out of here and we will have to find him on our own." Rob acknowledged the instructions with a nod of his head. They were on a porch and moved to the actual back door. Sam looked through the window sheer. He could see one large room with a kitchenette. Two doors were along the wall on the right. He judged one of them to be the bedroom. Their target was sitting watching T.V. on a recliner. Sam turned to Rob,

"Okay, listen up. We can remove the hinge pins and open this door from the side the locks are not on since it opens outward." Sam put some of the left over oil on the hinges and put the vial away. He found the hinges were not rusty because it was an inside door and there wasn't any paint on them. He worked on the hinges until the last one popped into his hand. The door moved just a tad creating a soft 'ting' sound. Their target looked toward the back door at hearing the sound. The boys froze. Their target went back to watching T.V. after he was satisfied no other sounds came.

Sam saw a screwdriver sitting on the window ledge near the outside door. He stuck it in the side of the door near the middle hinge and said to Rob,

"Okay, this is it. I'm going to pull this door open

and start walking fast toward this guy. I'll have my gun
on him. I want you to pay attention to the side doors and
rooms and watch my back. If anyone comes out of them
stick your gun right in their face and tell them to get on
the floor. I'll handle this guy we're after."

Then, with little hesitation, he wrenched open the
door and shoved it aside. As Sam started walking
through the kitchen he could see that this guy had no
idea what was going on. He started to get up but Sam
was already in front of him.

"Down on the floor shithead." Rob followed
stopping at each room. He looked inside and found no
one present.

"Face down on the floor." Sam said to their
target. The guy kept asking what they wanted.

"Shut up or I'll pop a cap in you. Where's the cash
and dope?" Sam asked. The guy said he didn't know
what he was talking about.

"Listen pal," said Sam. "You don't tell me what I
want to know and I'll shove this gun up your ass and pull
the trigger." The guy just laid there. Sam turned him
over and sat on him. He began beating him with the gun.
With his arms pinned by Sam's legs, there was nothing
he could do against the gun slamming into the skin of his
face. He started yelling,

"Okay, okay I'll tell you everything." Rob moved
closer while Sam was beating him and now had his gun
fixed on their target.

"Rob, hold your gun on him. Kill him if he moves
an inch. I'm going to find something to tie him up with,"
Sam said as he got off the target and went back into the
kitchen. Rob could hear all the drawers being open and
the contents tossed around. Sam found some duct tape
and brought it to the living room where the guy was still
flat on the floor. Sam tied the guy's hands and legs. Then
he went to the porch and took the clothes line down.

He tied some to his feet and then wrapped it twice around his neck and knotted it. The targets feet had been pulled up to the back of his head. This guy wasn't going anywhere.

There was a knock on the front door. Rob took a towel that was on the table and jammed it in the guy's mouth and then they both dragged him to the kitchen. Sam went to the front door and asked who was there. It turned out to be the landlady wondering about the noise. He answered that he had tripped but everything was alright. The landlady went away. Sam went back into the kitchen and slapped the target across the face.

"Where's the cash and dope," He asked. Rob pulled out the gag. "The cash is in the backpack in the closet," their target strained. "The dope is in the garage in the trunk of the car. You're not going to kill me, are you?" The guy was worried now. Rob went and got the cash. He saw only one stack was opened and judged that most of the money was there. Rob zipped the bag shut. Sam started asking more questions.

"Why did you run up here with the cash and dope?" Sam wondered if the guy had something to do with Felix.

"I have friends who deal big up here. I was going to meet them tomorrow and work out a deal for protection." He was straining every other word with his face between the cuffs of his pants.

"Where were you going to meet?" Sam was starting to get an idea.

"At a house on Addison Avenue the address is on the table." The guy thought the more info he gave, the better his chances.

"Why would they want to deal with you?" Sam asked.

"Because I have three keys of cocaine sitting in my car, which is what makes these people tick. The dope should buy me protection."

"How much do these guys deal?" Sam asked. His tone more civil now.

"More than you or I could do in a year's time. They do it every day," the guy answered.
Sam reached out and put his gun to the guy's chest. He pulled the trigger. The body shook for a second. Sam shot him once again in the head for good measure. The guy didn't move. Rob stared at the guy.

"Wow! I never thought you had it in you to do something like that, Sam." Which wasn't true. It was near one in the morning. They took the guy's keys and wiped down everything they remembered touching. Rob wiped down the back door. Sam looked at Rob when they had finished.

"I have a plan Rob and it is going to be dangerous. I hope you're up to doing it with me." Rob didn't respond at that moment. They left the house as fast as they could and made for the garage. The door was locked but they found the key that opened it on the guy's key ring. An old Chevy Malibu, in mint condition, sat in front of them. It was powder blue with a dark blue stripe running down the center of the body. They opened the trunk and found the keys of cocaine and two Mac 10 machine pistols. Sam thought this was a stroke of luck. The fact they had silencers on them was even more of a bonus. He began to wonder just what this guy actually had planned. Did the target need protection or was he trying to make himself a bit wealthier? The boys took the guns and stuffed them in the bag with the cash. The cocaine was already bagged in the guy's back pack so they grabbed that too. The boys took everything to their car and got in. Rob regarded Sam with some hesitation. Sam was breathing sort of heavy and he just killed a guy. Sam turned to Rob.

"Look, Rob. Here is what we are going to do.

We're going to meet these guys. We'll get them to take us inside their place. We're going to give them the cocaine for protection but when I unzip the bag and grab the machine pistol, I am going to try and kill everyone in the room. Your job will be to cover the door behind me. When we're done we'll take all their cash but leave their coke because cocaine never did anyone any good. We don't need to go down that road. Do you follow me, Rob?" Sam wanted to make sure there would be no mistakes.

"Yeah sure, Sam, should I take the safety off my Glock and the machine pistol? Also, tell me what we are going to do after that?" Sam looked at Rob. Chambered a round in his Glock and pointed it at the wall.

"We are going to find a nice place to stay for a day or so. Then we figure out where we can get our next gangland dose of cash. After we hit enough of them, we're going to go to Europe and spend the rest of our lives on the French Riviera. How does that sound?" Rob started to smile and even chuckled a bit.

"Sure Sam. That sounds okay to me."

Sam wasn't finished yet. He went on to tell Rob how they would go to the address and wait. They would watch who comes and who goes and how many there are. Perhaps it was the gang's headquarters but it could be a drop house too. Sam wanted to be sure. Sam wanted a big score because his lust for blood and money was beginning to stir in his mind. Military soldiers are trained to kill. They think it, live it, feel it and for some, they want it. Sam's greed was starting to take control.

The boys found a hiding place across the street from the address. It was an abandoned building waiting for demolition. On the third floor they could see through broken windows down to the house below. It looked like a normal lower middle-class home. The porch boards squeaked walking up to the door and the siding was rotting off the wall studs. There were many houses in similar condition on the street. At any one given time, for the time the boys were present, there were three people sitting or leaning on the porch. A car filled with people pulled up to the curb. Everyone got out, shut the doors, and went inside the house. They had been in the house for quite some time. Four of the people from the car came back out. They got in the car and took off down the street.

"I think this is where they keep their stash Sam," said Rob as he situated a shoulder along the window sill. He had to move a bit farther back because of the five foot round hole in the floor right in front of the window. "I've been watching the back. I can see between the houses to the yard. Three guys just left in another car down the alley. I can't tell if there are any more guys in the yard or by the back door though." The night was pitch black and there was little illumination from the street lights. Most were not working. It's a fair bet the energy company wasn't coming to this neighborhood any time soon to fix them.

Sam nodded his head.

"That's okay Rob. This is the place we want. Let's get a little sleep before we start some trouble." He let his back slide down the wall until his ass hit the floor. Rob did the same. He decided after this job he would get some decent clothes and a shower.

It was midnight. The moon fought scattered clouds that were moving north at a good clip. They woke up after two hours of sleep. They started again to case the front of the house. They lucked out in a way because these gangsters of the hood were confident in their location. It was doubtful that the cops would even come into this area. The boys also heard one guy ask another for some cash from his homey who said to ask Jared inside. This bit of information gave the boys a name they could use to pull off their heist.

The time on the paper for the meeting was one in the morning. Sam started running the steps through his mind. He wanted the cash to cover the gun so they could get in the front door. Then, once inside, he would give up the coke. It would be tested by one of the gang. At least they do on all the cop shows on TV. He would then ask for a safe house. When they asked him for the money he would put the bag on the table to dump it out. At the same time, he'd pull out the pistol and kill everyone in the room. He hoped Rob was up for his part or they both could end up dead. Sam didn't want to get shot in the back. Just the thought made him shiver. He went over the plan for Rob just before it was time to make the meeting.

The boys walked out of the gangway between the buildings and made their way across the street. An older teen got up off the front stair and walked up to them. He wore loose fitting clothes like he found them at a thrift store. His pants sagged down in the back, boxers showing the roundness of his ass. Sam couldn't figure how they could run from cops in a getup like that. He had deep blue eyes and a unibrow. He walked with authority.

"What you want here, dudes?" He asked, moving his eyes from one to the other of them. Sam was quite a bit taller than the kid and had to look down on him. A serious look jumped onto Sam's face.

"I have a meeting with Jared," he said still staring the kid down. The kid looked at what they were carrying.

"What's in the bags?"

"That belongs to Jared." Disbelief came over the kid's face.

"Open that one," the kid said, not taking his eyes off the bags. Sam put the bag on his knee and unzipped it. You could see the stacks of cash. Sam pretended that he was getting a bit bothered by all this question and answer shit. Another kid came out and stood on the porch.

"Is that good enough for you? Sam asked.

"No. Open the other one," he said. Sam reached back and changed bags with Rob. He put this bag on his knee and unzipped the zipper. He tilted it toward the kid.

"This is for Jared too. You going to let me in or do I have to go somewhere else?" Sam questioned a little smartly. He leaned a bit closer to the kid, invading his space. The kid backed up a bit and gave Sam and Rob a good looking over. He pointed to the door.

"Through the door, down the hall, last opening on the right.

"Thanks." Sam started for the stairs and began to climb them. Rob was close in tow. Sam mentally tallied four men outside. One of the gangsters opened the door for him and then closed it behind Rob. No one was present when they entered the house. The boss inside must have felt secure with just those outside guarding. They walked toward the back. Sam could see through the kitchen windows to the back porch. There was only one person there that he could see and he was looking right at him.

Sam stopped and turned right toward the doorway. His eyes fell on a room that was as long as the house. There were three guys and two girls. The girls were doing bumps of coke on a mirror between two Victorian chairs. Both had the shortest of shorts on and tiny blouses. Each blouse a different color with different flowers. One of the blonds had a girl's black leather vest. The guys were counting money on the table. One of the guys looked like he came straight out of a Bugs Moran mobster movie. He had a complete pin striped suit. This one, Sam thought, was their money man or banker. The other two wore loose clothes. They could have been vagrants.

The boss walked in from a little room off to the left. It wasn't a room, per se, more like a small parlor. As the boys stepped closer, Sam could also see a high backed king's chair and a gilded Louis the Fifteenth table, with a phone on it. The boss sat in an arm chair at the table with the three guys.

"So, you're the guy that contacted me about protection. I thought it was for only one person?" he said with a heavy Italian accent. His young face made him look more like a Diva than a Don.

"It took a few days to get here," Sam said. "I picked up a bodyguard so I could sleep."

"I suppose you have the right amount of cash?" The boss asked. Sam could see a bit of sparkle in his eye as if cash were king with this guy.

"Yes," said Sam, "but we need the cash. We were hoping you would agree to three keys of coke in payment. It's pure and uncut. I need most of my cash for transportation for when things blow over. I just need a safe haven where I can disappear for three months. The coke is worth three times the cash."

"Well now," said the boss. "Pedro, come and check this man's dope for me." The pin stripe suit got up and walked over to Sam. He told Sam to put the package on the table. Sam did as he was told. The suit pulled a Bowie knife from under his suit jacket and stuck the tip in one of the packages. He wet his finger, stuck it in the coke and then stuck it on his tongue. He opened his mouth, "It is pure, boss." The boss looked at Sam and nodded his approval.

"I'll need some upfront cash for the apartment. You okay with that?" The boss asked. Sam wanted nothing to go wrong.

"Sure," he said as he reached deep into the bag and pulled out the machine pistol. Things began to get serious at this point. Sam blasted away. He hit the boss first, who seemed to jump out of his seat and hit the wall. The sounds of the bullets leaving the gun were like a pencil eraser tapped on a wooden desk top. The first guy to his right caught a load or three in the belly and doubled over. The two other guys were reaching for their weapons. Sam nailed them in the chest, tipping them and their chairs over.

Both girls were reaching for guns they had stuck in their garter belts. One even got a shot off at Sam but it went wide of his head. He cut the girls almost in half. The only thing stopping him was the pistol had given up its ammo. Sam grabbed the other pistol out of the bag. He turned and saw Rob standing by an opening in the wall. He was looking down the hallway and back toward the porch. His Glock in hand. He was doing his job. The muffled sounds from the silencer directed no attention from the inside of the house. Sam called to Rob,

"Okay Rob, we have only a minute or two to find their stash.

They both ran around the room. Rob took the left side Sam the right. They were looking for a panel or secret opening. Maybe even a safe. They saw nothing. Finally standing in front of the small parlor Rob saw what looked like a half circle groove in the carpet. Upon further inspection they both figured the wall moved far enough to allow someone to walk behind it. Sam told Rob to push the wall while he stood ready with the machine pistol to level who ever may be inside. Rob pushed on the wall and it moved. It followed the semi-circle in the floor neatly. The interior was empty. Stacks of piled cash lined the shelves on one side and stacks of coke lined the other. There must have been over a million dollars in the room. There were bank bearer bonds, stock certificates and about fifteen keys of coke. The boys had found the jackpot. They also found some old bank money bags and started to stuff them with the cash. They didn't care about the coke. They had ten bags full.

"There is no way we're going to take this all at once. Let's call all the guys out front and tell them the boss wants them. When they get inside we can take them out. Then we can take out any that are in the back. After we do that Rob I want you to go get the car and drive it to the alley behind the house. I'll take care of things here and bring all this cash out to meet you."

So that's what they did. Rob went to the front door and told those on the porch the boss wanted them all inside. As the last guy walked by Rob, he closed the door and releasing the safety on his Glock, shot the last guy in the back of the head. Brain matter was flung to both sides of the hallway walls. He then shot the guy in front of him in the back. The first guy that walked in turned around with a gun in his hand. Sam riddled his back full of lead from the other end of the corridor.

"Damnit, Sam. What if you missed?" Rob's angry tone stung Sam. The possibility of Sam hitting Rob was great in this situation. Sam felt he was a pretty good shot and cocky about it too.

"There was no way Rob. Did you see the size of that guy? Now go get the car and bring it round to the back before somebody shows up for some blow." Sam locked the front door after Rob left to go get the car. He didn't want anyone dropping by when they were least expected. Rob saw there was no one in the street. It looked surreal, as if low clouds were floating in the street, backlit by the only working street light. It would take Rob about ten minutes to get the car and bring it around back. Sam grabbed the bank money bags and stuffed them into a thirty gallon garbage bag he found.

He began to drag it to the back door. A guy they had not seen before who was sitting just outside the back door got up when he heard Sam coming. He opened the back door and saw the bag.

"Let me help you with that. The boss must be moving again," said the guy. This guy was a flunky kept around for the heavy moving of dope. His arms looked like he could lift a car.

"Yes he is," said Sam. "He wants all this out by the gate. Somebody is coming to pick it up."

"Okay and since I am new here, I'll take the whole thing for the boss. Are we moving the dope too? He asked.

"Nope," said Sam. "The boss wants to keep the stash here for another week. We're just making a deposit. Get that down to the gate. I'll be there in a minute." The thug picked the bag up with both hands and threw it over his shoulder like someone would sling a backpack. The steps creaked as he went down them and moved toward the back gate. Sam went back in the boss's room and closed the moving doorway. He checked each of the people in the room to make sure they were dead. One of the girls made a noise. He walked over and shot her between the eyes. He took the credit cards the boss and suit had. He was trying to make it look like a robbery.

Sam picked up the empty machine pistol and threw it in the original bag of cash they brought. Stopping only to make sure all were dead. He walked back out the door. The wannabe thug was waiting by the gate with the thirty gallon bag. Sam walked up to him and asked if he could get the garage door open. The thug opened the door just as Rob stopped the car by the gate. Then the wannabe picked up the bag and put it in the trunk Rob clicked open from inside the car. The wannabe said,

"I've never seen the boss with this car before."
Sam plugged him in the back of the head and dragged
his body into the garage. He weighed a ton. It took both
the boys to get him in. They re-locked the garage door.
Sam got into the passenger side of the car and told Rob
to get the hell out of there. Rob punched the gas and the
car lifted from the torque of the engine. The tires
squealed down the alley leaving burn marks on the
asphalt.

Chapter Four

Marshal Carl Oscar Barrington, also known as Cob, had been a Marshal for close to fifteen years. His ability to catch the bad guys was a legend at the academy. Cob always got his man. He wasn't perfect. He'd probably forget his own anniversary if he wasn't reminded. To him work came first. He was a family man with two kids. His son, who was ten and into soccer, was good at school. His daughter who was fourteen, well, she was fourteen and there were boys involved. It wasn't easy for her to have boyfriends. She was known as the po po's daughter at school. She had friends none the less. For Cob, nothing was too good for his kids. Even when his work load was heavy, he managed to make it to those very important games and plays. Most of the time anyway. Today the kids were into their own thing. It seemed that they were growing up and becoming more independent.

Cob was in charge of the gangland area of the city. He oversaw the narcotics and homicide divisions.

Cob wasn't new in this area. Many of his friends were in gangs and some he had had to put away for life. Chicago had been infiltrated by drugs, extortion for protection, and gang wars since the sixties. It seemed every time they would take down a new gang leader, another would sprout up like a weed. Cob's division was one of the best. It carried armor, weapons, gas, and a thing called steadfastness. They always found their man. Everyone on the team would see their job through. The team actually received Hummers. They served overseas in Army battles. Their armor was intact and it helped them to roll right into the middle of a gang fight. It allowed them to break it up with less danger to life. Then they could more easily catch the people involved.

Cob's office was in the building next to the FBI on Michigan Avenue. It wasn't big and it was missing a lot of windows. Cob would say 'what the hell is there to look at, the sky?' to anyone who would listen. Cob was a simple man. He had a black belt in Karate and Judo. He was a marksmen with an uncanny sense of where to find his perp.

On this day the Captain came into Cob's office.

"Cob we have a problem. Something big is going down on the northwest side. Local boys found a corpse in the upstairs apartment of a small house. He was shot in the head and chest close range. Definitely gangland style. His ankles were tied to his neck."

"What the hell are the gangs doing on the north side of town? Cob demanded. The captain perched himself on the corner of Cob's desk. He lit a smoke.

"I have no idea. That's why I'm giving you the case. The local boys over there don't know who's who in gangland so get over there and figure this out. Keep me informed of what you find. The Mayor is starting to get curious again. I don't want him breathing down my neck." Cob noticed the tenseness in the man's voice.

"Okay Cap," said Cob. "I'll get Dawn and we'll go see what's up." Cob got up and grabbed his coat, slapped a hat on his head, and walked out of the office. He stopped downstairs in the break room and saw Dawn clamping her teeth into a giant sub sandwich. He stuck his head through the doorway,

"Hey! Is anyone going to put a leash on that Tasmanian devil or at least put a lock on the frig?" A big smile spread across his face. Dawn swallowed what she had just bit off the sandwich. Her face became a grotesque whirl of anger like she might burst the vein that became evident on her neck.

"Up yours, Cob." That said, she put down her sandwich, and shot him a bird, double barrel.

"Come on Dawn," said Cob. He walked closer toward where Dawn was sitting. "Finish up we have a job to take care of out on the north side." He knew she had family out that way which prompted Dawn to say,

"The north side?" Dawn declared. "My aunt lives out there. She says nothing ever exciting happens there."

"Where does she live at out there?" Cob asked.

"She's just off Irving Park Road and Western Avenue. She has a bungalow behind a small factory," said Dawn.

"We can stop and pay her a visit," he suggested. "The place we're going to is quite close." He did not tell Dawn he thought this might be a random killing rather than something gang related. He disagreed with what the Captain said. The local boys could most likely handle it. Dawn shoved what was left of her sub-sandwich in the trash. She grabbed her coat off the chair and headed out the break room door with Cob. It was April in Chicago so the temperatures outside were still a little brisk. The six-foot snow banks were gone and children were back to hard floor games. The local boys club off Irving Park

Road had been packed.

Dawn was a veteran cop who had just became a marshal. She had long blond hair, green eyes, long legs and muscle. She beat up half the guys who went through the academy with her and she wasn't afraid of anything. Plenty of people, including her captain, thought that she might get killed with an attitude like that. If anyone confronted her or worried about her, she would say 'you gotta go if it's your time to go.' Dawn didn't like to drive so she sat shotgun. She thought about her aunt but figured she hardly left the house unless it was with her. She was hoping there wasn't any new gang activity starting out there. It was pretty far from the city center. Cob was filling her in on the way.

"Okay partner. I'm told what we have is a dead guy in an apartment next to a bowling alley." She turned her head towards him,

"That's Waveland Bowling Alley. I spent lots of time there when I was younger," she said to Cob.

"Any gang activity you know of out there?" Cob questioned. Her response was quick,

"No. You have the neighborhood kids causing trouble now and then. You might get a jacked battery call on occasion. The locals pick them up in a hurry. Most of the local cops live in the neighborhood. They all grew up with the ones who make the trouble. Once the parents got the kids off to college they were usually okay."

Cob and Dawn took Irving Park Road up from the lakefront and turned left at Western Avenue. They made the trip to the Bowling Alley on Western in less than two minutes. They parked in a space across from the house in the bowling alley parking lot. The locals had the street blocked off. They came up to the front of the house and found a local cop talking to an older woman. The old women finished talking. Cob walked up to the cop and asked,

"Who is this nice lady? The officer pulled his writing pad out of his upper pocket.

"This is Mrs. Steerwell, marshal. She owns the house and was renting to the victim." Cob directed his attention to the woman.

"Hello, Mrs. Steerwell. I'm Marshal Barrington and this is Marshal Thorn. We would like to ask you a few questions if you don't mind." Mrs. Steerwell was looking bit fragile from all the commotion. People were running around the house.

"Not at all detective, now like I was saying to the other officer..." She finished her story telling to Cob and Dawn. Cob asked a few more questions and then decided it was time to see the room. The print and polish people had finished what they do best at crime scenes and told Cob and Dawn it was all theirs. The local dicks were told to stay out of it so they just watched the two marshals. They walked into the room and Cob said,

"You know, this is already looking a bit funny to me. If you're going to shoot a guy why tie him up? Unless you're trying to get information out of him." Dawn noticed and made mention that there were no family pictures around. They checked his person and found a wallet with two hundred dollars in it. Cob didn't think it was a robbery. There also wasn't a fight. The guy's face was a bit torn up. The landlady didn't say anything about hearing shots or a struggle. No one ransacked the place looking for something. Cob looked over at one of the cops and asked,

"Hey my friend, will you tell the coroner to send up this guy's clothes to my office when they're finished with them? Cob liked to do his own research during a case.

"Sure thing marshal, I'll let them know right away," the officer replied. Cob found Dawn in the kitchen.

"Well Cob, looks like a break in, so he may not have known his killer. And look at this." She pointed to the string tied to bells on the back porch. "What do you make of this string arrangement?" Cob went and pulled on the string and bells hanging in one corner by the ceiling began to make a racket.

"Well, it's not Mozart. I think this guy was expecting somebody he didn't want to see. Let's run a trace on this guys prints and see where he comes from. Would you call down to narcotics and see if they have anything on him when we get his personals?" Cobb always tried to cover the bases. He had a feeling this was no ordinary killing.

"Sure Cob, and while I'm at it, I'll have ballistics check the shells for prior use." She left out of the room with Cob following shortly after. They got back in the car and Cob stamped on the gas. The rear of the car shook side to side before finally straightening out in the middle of the street. Cob thought while he was driving that there was something suspicious about this crime. It was similar to another he worked but he couldn't remember where it was. He knew it was back in L.A. but where exactly.

L.A. was a rotten town back in the seventies. Cripps and Bloods always feuding. The general Hispanic gangs making a name for themselves. It was hell for the force. There were always turf wars. Every night somebody ended up dead or hurt. Neighborhood dumpsters were checked regularly before being picked up. You have no idea what happens to a body when it's crushed in a garbage truck. It wasn't only kids doing the gangbanging either. Kids back then grew to be the bosses of the future. It was something to look forward to. A boss didn't have to do much. He gave orders and he always had a steady flow of cash, girls and drugs.

Eight year old kids selling crack on the streets did not appeal to Cob. The fact that they also carried a piece stuffed in the folds of their loose fitting pants made him cautious. He hated dealing with calls for domestic abuse back then. The young acted as a buffer for the older bosses. They would carry out the killings or be killed. If caught, they would bide their time in juvie, until they could escape or be released. Either way, the gang made sure they had anything they wanted while behind bars. In L.A., it wasn't about getting out of the ghetto, it was about staying in the ghetto and moving up in the ranks. The more Cob pushed his memory trying to connect the one incident to the other. He felt it slipping away the harder he thought about it. Dawn yelled,

"Cob, look out!" She grabbed the wheel and yanked it toward her side of the car. Cob saw in the driver's side rear view mirror a semi-tractor inching by his window in slow motion. The tractor-trailer scratched the upper part of the window molding just as Dawn moved the wheel.

"Cob, what the hell were you thinking?" Asked Dawn, a bit irritated. Cob let out a breath of air and said,

"That's just it Dawn." He checked all his mirrors and the traffic around him. "I was thinking." He pulled into the slow lane and let off the gas.

Chapter Five

Sam and Rob drove all that night and got a room in Indianapolis. They went into the room and took all the money bags with them. Rob loosened the ties and emptied them out on the bed. He began to count how much was in one banded stack while Sam gathered all the stacks together on the room table. There were forty stacks and the one Rob had in his hands. Rob found there were ten thousand in each stack. Rob looked at Sam and asked,

"What are we going to do with all this cash?" Rob thought they might get robbed themselves.

"Well let's see," said Sam. "The first thing we're going to do is store it. I mean we are going to put it in a safe deposit box. We need two things. The first is a private investigator to find out where the gang's headquarters are in this city. Then we need to find some fake ID's. After that, we can find a mobile home park and buy an old beat up trailer where no one will look for us. I think we should work our way to Miami.

We'll have freedom to go from there to anywhere in the world."

The next day under clear skies they sat in massive traffic jams. The boys found an out of the way trailer park. They haggled with the manager on the price of a two-bedroom home in the back of the park. Sam wanted it out of sight if they could help it. The manager noted there was a hole in the roof over the second bedroom. He did say the rest of the home was fine.

"I can have my repair guy come and fix it for you at my cost?" The manager suggested.

"No thanks. We have a friend in the construction business," Sam replied. They settled on three-thousand cash for the home as-is. Sam felt it was a good deal. He had seen a few trailers the same size going for about nine-thousand. The trailer wasn't in that bad a shape and the weather looked to be good for the time they expected to stay in town. The water ran and the electric only cost seventy-five a month according to the manager. Sam made the decision to put three hundred ninety thousand in safe deposit boxes. They closed all the curtains in the house and dumped the cash on the table. They both started to separate the cash into one hundred thousand dollar packs. Sam said,

"Rob, why don't you finish counting for me. I saw an office supply store down the street where I can pick up a few attaché cases we can put the money in to get it to the bank. It'll look more formal that way." Sam felt a rumble in his stomach. "I'll stop and get us something to eat on the way back."

"Okay Sam, but no hamburgers," Rob demanded.

"Oh, what size are you Rob," Sam asked. "I think I'll stop at a store and get us some jeans. I still have bloodstains on what I am wearing. Let me have your jacket too. Wow!" Sam exclaimed looking at his shirt.

"Do you think the manager saw the stains?"

"Nope, with all that dirt it looks like you're a car mechanic, but take my jacket anyway," Rob suggested. "The manager might have thought it was paint. I'm a size 34 long in pants. Just get me a large shirt with short sleeves." He hoped Sam would get nice stuff. Sam left after writing a few notes.

Dark clouds rolled in about two hours later. It smelled like rain, but the TV said only twenty percent chance. Rob had stacked one hundred thousand dollars in four separate piles. He thought this to be a lot of money but it didn't feel like he was rich. They were putting it in a bank. It didn't feel like he could do anything he wanted. Rob knew they would be on the run now and wondered what plans Sam had. He also thought about Tabitha and her father. Rob thought that maybe Sam was trying to prove something to his uncle. Sam thought that they had a week or so before the people in Tampa started to wonder what's going on and where they were. They should have returned by now. Those people were going to be pissed. About an hour passed and Sam came in the front door carrying a bunch of bags.

"Hey Rob, here's a sub sandwich for you. I rented a garage and paid six months in advance to store the Mercedes. I picked up the attaché cases. Here, start loading up the cash so we can get to a bank and get rid of it." Sam held up a plaid shirt. "Do you like this one?" He asked. "I got it on sale. I have a solid colored one if you want. If you don't like it we can take them back." Sam was trying to be diplomatic since clothing is a personal thing. Rob turned and looked over both shirts.

"Wow! That one," Rob said pointing to the plaid one. "will wake you up in the morning. At least it's blue plaid." Sam moved over to the table. Rob took the shirt.

"I have a lead on getting us new ID's," said Sam.

"I also bought a Chevy Monty Carlo that runs great. It has a beefed up 305 in it. There's a bank down the road about a mile or so. I figured we could dump our first load there. From there we can continue down the street to the next three we see."

"Sam, if we are going to Miami," Rob asked, "why are we leaving all the cash in this town? I mean it's not like we can grab it and spend it, especially if it's not in an account?" Sam turned to look at Rob and thought *man when is this dude going to get it together with his thinking*. So Sam said,

"Oh c'mon Rob, think! What if we're stopped for a traffic violation and the cops open the trunk and then start opening the bags? How would we explain that? We need a place to crash where we can be inconspicuous. No one would expect us to have this kind of cash and stay in a place like this. Also my friend, once we get settled and the heat dies down we can just fly up here and get the cash out. I will have copies of the box keys made for you too. We're going to make a lot more cash before we get the cash out. We'll have boxes in every town on the way to Miami. Now we need to find a place to get some ammo and extra clips for these guns. Oh, and by the way, if we were to get an account they would trace that to us if we get caught. If we do have to do some time the money will be there when we get out. No one cares what you put in a safety deposit box." Rob didn't like the tone his partner was spewing,

"I'm still a little freaked out by you killing people and now I'm a killer. I know it was what you had to do but it still bothers me. That dude did not have to die in my opinion. I understand these guys are dirt bags and get little kids hopped up on dope. How many more jobs do you want to do?" Rob was trying to be sensible in his own mind and come to grips with the situation. Sam replied with a brood grin,

"I figure we can do well here. Then take the money to Kentucky and deposit it. Do well there and take the money to Jacksonville and from there head to Miami and lay low. If we don't run into any problems, the whole plan should be a wiz." Rob looked Sam straight in the eye,

"What if one of us gets shot or even killed?"

"Well then," said Sam, "the other knows where the money is. The boxes will have both our names on them and then whoever it is can go and lay low until everything blows over. You're not bailing out on me now are you Rob?" Sam wasn't worried if that's what Rob wanted to do. He needed Rob to help with the jobs and hoped he would say the right thing.

"No Sam, I was just thinking of Tabitha and her father is all," Rob said with a worried expression on his face. Sam decided it was time to tell him about his Uncle Felix especially since it would clear up certain thoughts in Rob's head. Sam began,

"Rob. Did I ever tell you about the time Felix beat me silly? He was the one who found me and Marcie together in the shed. Marcie's dad is my uncles best friend. He put me in the hospital for four days. He hit me with a shovel Rob and then with a garden rake. Why do you think my little finger is so bent? The doctors couldn't fix it right because of the amount of damage he did." While Sam spoke, he was reliving that time.

"Then why did we go down to see him in the first place? Asked Rob defiently.

"Because I wanted to go south and I needed to have a place to stay. I was low on cash and Nana's cooking is awesome."

"I can agree with that. The girls were kinda funny too. You know, when I went downstairs after you took off, I found a passage underground between the houses. It was my finding the door that brought Tabitha and me together. I mean, she caught me watching the people make coke bags and we sort of hit it off. I suppose I am carrying a family secret now. I know she wanted to be with us but I also know that it is better she is not. I would hate for anything to happen to her. She's a good girl Sam."

"I agree, Rob. She is a nice girl. She is better off away from us for now, but let's get this job done and see if we can't set ourselves up so we don't have to work. Then you can take care of Tabby the way she should be taken care of." Sam went to the kitchen. He discarded the bags from the stores into the trash. He had'nt realized he still carried them.

"Okay so what's next?" Rob asked. Sam stood there and thought a second. He put a hand on Rob's shoulder.

"Okay, let's get the cash in the safety deposit boxes. I'll call a private investigator and then see if this guy I ran into can do good ID's. We'll have to find a place to get ammo for these guns." Rob had filled the attaché cases by the time Sam had finished talking. There was a few thousand dollars left over from the even amounts in the attaches. They split the cash and left the house in good spirits.

Chapter Six

It was a bright morning, too bright for Cob. It was one of those days where you spilled coffee on your shirt. Or said all the wrong things to your wife before you went out the door. Cob didn't have time for yard work right now. This was not just another Saturday and Cob had real work to do. He took the long way to work while reflecting on what happened earlier at home.

His attention shifted to L.A. Something happened during a case while he was on patrol. He just couldn't grasp what it was. In that instance, two guys were imitating in real life what they saw on TV. They were partners in crime. The problem was the police didn't know there were two of them doing the crimes. They never could find anything that linked one to the other. Then these two took off through a field, muddy from a previous rain, and left imprints of their shoes. The cops put it together that the criminals carried each other for about a hundred steps. They would then split in two directions. As it turned out, witnesses placed the two in the field, the tracks left were from the same shoes sold at all the shoe stores. All the tracks confirmed the weight. This information didn't help his current case at all.

Cob walked through the door to his office. His cell phone began to ring. The captain was sitting on the couch with his cell phone to his ear.

"Don't bother that's me on the other end." Cob checked anyway.

"Hello, cap. What can I do for you today?"

"Cob. We have another homicide about two miles east of Wrigley Stadium on Addison Avenue. It's in the ghetto blocks."

"Ghetto blocks. I thought we had cleaned that place up two years ago." Cob remembered bullet proof vests torn to pieces during a raid on the neighborhood. They managed to get rid of gang violence at least for a while.

"Well this one will get your heart running," the Chief advised. " Ten people dead. The locals have the place locked down for a block in all directions. Nobody is talking. The FBI is getting involved so be careful. We don't want any out of bounds trouble on this one. Try to be nice." Cob had been known for doing whatever it took to solve a case. He was also known for not dealing well with the FBI. They always shoved their importance on things. They were stuffy people. And those suits they wore made them look like CIA or movie characters.

"Okay cap. I'll grab Dawn and we'll go take a look. We're also going back to the other site. I want to look around more over there," Cob advised.

"Alright," the captain agreed, "but keep me informed. I'm the only thing that stands between you and the commissioner. You take care of yourself, Cob." The captain shook Cob's hand and left the office. Cob grabbed his coat and walked out to the stairs. His feet hitting the stairs sounded like a machine pistol echoing through the stairwell. On the second floor, he went through the door and found Dawn back in the break room, working on a doughnut. A grin melted across his face.

"You know. I just don't understand how you can stuff yourself and never gain any weight. What's your secret, partner?" Dawn was a muscular girl but she had a slender waist and agility. Police training took her to the next level of tomboy yet she still didn't seem to gain weight. Dawn smiled then and said,

"I have high metabolism, partner. You get any leads from forensics?" She asked him. She wanted to get back to business before any other jokes popped into Cob's mind.

"No. The casings were clean and the guy's clothes gave up no information. I want to go back and take a look at that place right after we check out this new job. It seems somebody went nuts killing ten people. All drug related, I'll bet, and get this it's in the ghetto blocks."

"The ghetto blocks were..."

"Cleared out a few years ago," Cob finished her sentence for her. "You were a member of that team I remember. Now, we need to get there and take a look. The feds are getting involved also so be on your best behavior. At least that's what the captain says. Maybe we'll get a raise if we catch the perp." Dawn rolled her eyes as she did every time the captain came up in conversation. They were two partners on the same wavelength.

"From your mouth to God's ears." Dawn replied.

Dawn snatched her coat from the hanger at the door and swung it on. They were in the car and on the road in less than three minutes. Cob was driving and he was in a hurry. Cob was thinking, as he always did while driving, that eleven people were murdered. These cases

were going big time fast. They didn't even know if the
first murder was related to the second massacre. He
thought there had to be motive for killing ten people at
one time. It had to be gang related or one was making its
move for more turf. It could also be an internal problem
where someone wanted to move up the ranks to leader.
They reached the house where the killings took place.
The print and polishers had left. Cob couldn't remember
when he started calling forensics those names. It fit their
job duties. The front door was open and they had to step
between the bodies that took up most of the floor space.
Cob looked at one of the local cops and asked,

"Do we know any of these people?"

"Not these," the officer replied, "but we know
all them in the other room." They walked down the hall.
Cob walked behind Dawn. Dawn glanced in the rooms
on the left before they reached the edge of the kitchen
and the entryway to the largest room in the house on the
right. Cob rounded the corner and was surprised. The
wall behind the card table looked like a piece of art. The
blood splatters rose in an almost planned pattern.
Almost like an artist painting a red cosmos. Three bodies
lay on top of each other and another was between the bar
edge and the wall. Two girls were on the floor. One with
a chair on top of her belly. Blood was scattered all over
the room and furniture. The same cop they talked with
earlier came into the room.

"There's another," he said pointing toward the
back of the house, "out in the garage. He took a bullet in
the head and was dead instantly according to forensics."
This officer liked Cob. Some of Cobs exploits had made it
into the academy. He was well known as the Marshal
who always gets his man.

"Thanks Mac," Cob turned inquiringly. "Hey
Mac, take a look at this room and tell me what you see."

"A lot of blood sir," replied Mac.

"I know that," Cob said agitated, "but humor me. What do you think happened here?"

"Well, I would say the perpetrator stood about here in front of the table with a machine gun. Then he sprayed the whole lot of them. He started with the guys in the chairs and moved to the girls. I think the girls stumbled trying to get out of the chairs. They were caught by surprise after seeing the guys get blasted. Otherwise they would have died in the chairs. Unless they used hollow point ammo which would give a much bigger kick upon entry." Cob listened satisfied with the assumption.

"That's a plausible situation. Thanks much, Mac. Would you go tell the coroner that he can have the three by the front door?"

"You betcha, Marshal." Mac left the room and went to the porch exiting out the back door. Cob turned and looked at Dawn.

"Dawn, what do you think happened here?" Cob was searching for something. He was looking for something that made sense. Some instinctive knowledge to lock his mind on what was happening.

"You want my professional opinion?" She asked. Dawn was being a smart ass and Cob knew it. She saw the serious look on his face and continued, "I agree with Mac only I think the person who did this was not a hardened killer." Hearing this stopped Cob in the middle of his thought. He gave her his undivided attention.

"What do you mean not a hardened killer?" Cob asked.

"Well," she said, "if you're a killer, you would shoot these guys and then stop and turn your body to take care of the girls. In this case here, the bullets start at the table and follow along the room from left to right. Our killer shot the whole left corner of the room before he would have come close to hitting the girls. This gave them time to try and get out of the chairs. Not to mention, the first girl was shot in the side and back. That tells me she was not facing her killer."

"That is perceptive Dawn and I agree. Let's go see the guy out back," Cob said as he started walking out of the room. He turned back to Dawn, "You know, it's about time Jared Bishop and his flunkies took some lead. That guy has been a real pain in my ass for years now. I wonder who will replace him." Jared Bishop was the head investigator for the FBI. Dawn shrugged her shoulders.

When they got to the garage, they looked in and saw a young man, a pool of blood on the floor around his head. He was lying near the back tire of an old forty-nine Nash. He was shot once in the head. Blood pooled on the floor. There was a blood trail leading from the alley to the garage that indicated that he was not shot in the garage itself. Cob asked a local cop to get some info from the neighbors but he knew it would lead to little information. No one talked in this area. Snitches don't live long around here. He noticed two foot prints in the dirt.

"Did forensics get plaster casts of these," he asked. She shrugged her shoulders.

"I don't know, but I'll call and ask." She started dialing her cell. After a minute or two of talking she said, "Forensics found a match between the casings here and those from the house by the bowling alley. They're sending a guy back to take the castings for the shoes." Cob found this information intriguing.

"Well now. That means we are dealing with the same perp and one, who in just a half day, graduated from killer to mass murderer. Let's get back to the office and see what else they have come up with. I wonder why the Feds aren't here. This is right up their alley. Maybe it's a jurisdiction problem or they're letting us play the first innings so they can win the game in the end. Damn Feds." Dawn rolled her eyes at the mention of the Fed's. They combed the yard and surrounding area for an hour or so and came up with nothing. They did the same to the house.

Chapter Seven

The clouds had moved off leaving an aquatic sky. The sun's orange spikes stabbing at the wavering day rose in the east. The rains had passed for at least four days according to the news. Local reports said nothing about Chicago. After Rob put all the money in the cases, Sam called a private investigator. He agreed to meet him about an hour after Sam would meet with Raphael. Raphael was the Hispanic immigrant he ran into outside a local store. He discussed purchasing ID's. He wanted to meet in the back of a grocery store not far away. They pulled up to the back door and honked once. Raphael came out and walked to the window of the car.

"Okay Gringoz, whatchew want exactly," he said.

"We need new driver's licenses and social security cards," replied Sam. He didn't care much for this guy but they needed the ID's to get the deposit boxes.

"For chew both iz gonna get expenzive gringo. Like I told you before, I make the best. Chew want to go in bar or cross border?" Raphael asked. He was trying to make extra cash off someone in a hurry. Sam was getting a bit angry listening to this bullshit questioning. A guy made a set for Sam in peoria Illinois for fifty dollars.

"How much are the ones for crossing the border?" Sam asked.

"Chew pays me two hundred each for licenze and one hundred each for social." Sam knew this was highway robbery, especially as they wouldn't be good for traveling, or if they got stopped. He was using the names of dead people Sam guessed. The boys did come into a lot of cash recently and they could afford it.

"How long will it take?" Sam asked. He did want to keep moving toward Miami as fast as possible.

"Tomorrow," said Raphael. "We meet here." Raphael took a camera out of his pocket. "Please get against the wall over there." The boys got out of the car and moved to the wall. They saw a large white square which they presumed was used often for the taking of these pictures. After a few flashes, Sam reached into his pocket and took out his wallet. He took out two one hundred dollar bills and handed them to Raphael.

"This is for you to start the job. You'll get the rest when you produce perfection. That okay with you?" Sam asked.

"Sure gringo, iz okay with me. I see chew tomorrow, right here, six at night." The boys watched him walk into the store. They both agreed he was working there as a stock boy. Management did not seem his forte. Sam didn't trust this guy at all.

"We may have lost two hundred dollars." Sam rumbled. "I don't trust him. I mean he just met me and he's taking my cash for a job. I wonder if he is a cop."

Rob started to walk back to the car and said,

"I think he's okay. At any rate, you wouldn't have found anyone else this quick around here. He might just run this whole area as far as ID's are concerned. Did you see how many Hispanic people lived in our trailer park?"

"You might be right Rob."Sam said.

"Are you sure this investigator should know what we're looking for?" Rob asked. "I mean, those jobs we did up there are on the news right now. My heart is still beating fast." Sam gave Rob a look of understanding. He thought to himself, what a time for you to start thinking like a criminal.

"You know me better than that Rob. I always have a plan. I'm just going to say all the right things to this investigator. By the time I am done he will almost give me what I want for nothing. Let's go see this guy now and get it over with." Rob sat behind the wheel and punched the pedal to the floor. The car lurched once and took off down the street.

The meeting place they set up was only a few blocks away. The investigator's name was Joel Montgomery. He was an ex-cop of twenty-two years on the Indianapolis Inner City beat. He was skinny and wore a trench coat and hat like Sherlock Holmes. This guy sported a nice Cuban cigar instead of the Mirshaum pipe Holmes was best known for. An illegal cigar at that. Rob parked the car in front of the restaurant and the boys went in. Sam put on his Budweiser hat so that the PI would know it was him. They ordered some sodas. About five minutes passed and a skinny guy walked in the door. Sam saw him first because he was facing the door. He also knew it was the right guy because a gun hung holstered under his left arm pit. Sam touched Rob's leg with his foot under the table and announced in a whisper that the guy was there. Mr. Montgomery saw the hat and sat down next to Rob. He sat half in and half out of the seat.

"So what do you two want me to do?" The PI asked. "I'm especially good with cheaters and missing persons and I can find out who your real father or mother are."

"No," said Sam. "It's not like that. We want to know where a group of people hang out and if possible, where there headquarters or clubhouse is located." A bit of suspicion ran across the guys face.

"And just who are these people you're looking for," asked Montgomery.

"We want to know where the dope dealers are. The ones that deal in crack and heroin and fight with rival gangs," replied Sam.

"What do you want those kinds of people for? I could tell you where they are for free, but it's your life going in their neighborhood." Sam put on his best sad face.

"Well, you see, we are from Chicago and recently my sister got involved with these gangsters and now is, we think, stuck on one of the guys in the gang. We tracked her down here. I am going to kidnap her from these dirtbags and bring her back home to mom. My mom is going crazy worrying about her and it's been four weeks now." Sam poured it on.

"I'll tell you what. I'll find out where the main clubhouse is for the largest gang in town. They're the only ones who do any traveling. I'll find out who is in charge also and I'll only charge you one hundred dollars. I can't stand it when they get nice people involved in their shit. Let's meet here tomorrow same time." The boys agreed and watched Mr. Montgomery leave the restaurant. Sam looked at Rob with a shit eaten grin on his face.

"Man, I told you he would help us. He usually gets five hundred dollars for retainer." Rob slapped Sam on the shoulder and lit a smoke.

"I have to tell you Sam, you sure know what you're doing. That acting was masterful. Pretty soon, we can roll ourselves out of a trailer and into a nice house somewhere."

"There's more where that came from Rob. It's about time we had our share."

The boys lounged around the trailer after stopping for some beer. They ordered a pizza which took forty minutes to arrive. Rob was looking out the kitchen window which showed a view straight down the main street of the park. The fronts of the trailers were spaced in almost perfect lines on either side. He saw a couple of girls yelling at each other in the living room two trailers down the street. He couldn't see well because they were on an angle facing the street. Their trailer backed up against the trailer court fence and looked down the street. He was sure neither one had a bra on. Rob opened up the front door.

"Where are you going?" Sam asked eyes slitted. Rob was getting a little tired of answering to Sam, but he let it go.

"I'm just checking out these two chicks down the street. I thought I saw them without bras on." This piqued Sam's interest and he said,

"Well if they look good bring them back here, okay?" Rob was thinking the same thing. Of course he also thought about Tabitha just then too.

"Yeah sure Sam, anything for you buddy." Rob walked down the street. He could hear the girls yelling at each other. It seemed to him that one of the girls stole the other's boyfriend. The girls had moved into the living room closer to the front window and Rob was standing right there. He got a real good look at them too. They appeared to be twins. Rob found it hard to tell the two apart except one was shorter than the other. One of the girls turned her head and saw Rob.

"Why don't you take a picture, it will last longer, you pervert!" She exclaimed. The acid in her voice dumbfounded Rob. He didn't realize he was in plain view. He didn't know what to do and he didn't want to upset them any more than they already were. *What if they called the cops?* He thought. He couldn't move his legs. A second or two passed and he yelled back,

"I thought you might like to have a beer or something." She replied, the anger on her face changing almost immediately, softer and more sexy.

"Who me?" she said in a pleasing voice.

"Or her," her voice changed like the low rumble before an earthquake.

"Well, I have a friend at the house. You can both come if you want." The girls looked at each other and then back at Rob. Rob was scratching the left side of his leg and he noticed the palms of his hands were starting to sweat. What he felt and had with Tabitha was quite different from what was transpiring here.

After what seemed like hours the girls began to put on tank tops and moved to what must have been the front entry to the house. They came from around a corner of the house. They both sported smiles now. The taller one also had larger breasts. As they approached him he could tell they were twins except for height and boobs. The short one came up to Rob,

"Hi. You can call me Stacy and this," pointing at her twin, "is Beth." They each grabbed one of Rob's arms and Beth said, "You're kinda cute, what's your name, handsome?" Rob told them his name and motioned with his head down the street toward their trailer.

"We live at the end there," Rob offered. We just moved in this morning. They all walked down to the boy's trailer. As they walked Stacy went first because Beth was hanging all over Rob slowing him down.

"So what's your friend like Rob?" Stacy asked. Her curious look belied the fact that her twin was already wanting Rob.

"Oh Sam's okay. We do a lot of things together," said Rob, "so we decided to just live together." Rob hoped he wouldn't give anything away about their situation. He hoped he wouldn't accidentally say the wrong thing. Then Stacy asked,

"What do you guys do for work? I mean. most everyone in this court works at the factory but we haven't seen you there. On Thursdays we work at the Four F Club." They entered the boy's trailer just as Stacy was asking Rob her question. Sam was nowhere to be seen. Just then, the flush of a toilet was heard. Sam came out into the living room.

"Sam, this is Beth," Rob said pointing to the taller girl, "and this is Stacy. She was just asking what we do for work. Actually, they want to know about you."

"Oh, hello ladies," said Sam. He looked them both over while opening the frig. The girls giggled at being called ladies. "Rob and I work together doing financial data recovery for a computer business. You both want a beer?" He produced three beers from the frig, carried them back to the girls and Rob, and then went back for his.

"Sure thing," replied Beth. "Computer work sounds boring."

"Staring at a screen all day and having to type like the wind," Stacy added. They moved to the couch and sat down placing their drinks on the ornate country style coffee table. Sam started a different conversation.

"So girls, you go to school near here?" Asked Sam.

"No way, we gave that up for dancing. We work at the factory and the Four F Club," she stated. Rob had no idea what that meant.

"What does the four F's mean? He asked. "I have heard of the Four H Club before," he stated a bit confused. Both girls started to laugh.

"No silly," Stacy's smile almost turning into a laugh. "the four F's are find um, feel um, fuck um, forget um, you should know that. It's just about the male motto." Rob felt a bit stupid, but he had never heard of that before.

Sam got up and pulled two more beers out of the frig. He handed one to Stacy who was sitting next to him on the couch and the other to Beth, then he went back and got two more for Rob and himself. He handed a beer to Rob. Rob appeared to have little experience with women as far as Sam could tell. He chalked it up to lack of the right kind of childhood experiences. Sam had learned from stolen magazines and sex videos his friend had come up with. Not to mention being the high school quarterback and all the cheerleaders he had. Now that he thought of it he was amazed none of those girls talked much about their experiences. He had had sex with at least eight of the fourteen girls. For Rob it was a bit different since he was not athletic.

Rob had an aptitude for math and art. He spent much of his time at home when he was younger. He had friends but they wanted to be engineers and architects like their fathers. Even his best friend whose father was a doctor could fix any kind of scrape, cut or bruise his friends would get when they did try to have daring adventures. Rob grew distant with his family who constantly hovered over his every move. Finally he ran off in search of life. Rob had few experiences with girls, which is why he felt a little sad that Tabitha wasn't there. He was also thinking about how he would feel if he spent time with Beth. She was damn good looking.

Stacy grabbed the remote and turned on the TV. She found a movie while flicking through the channels.

It looked to be a love story at first glance.
Rob got up and grabbed six beers out of the frig. His
hands were bigger than Sam's were. He enjoyed showing
off in front of Sam when he could. He brought them to
the table and plunked them down. Everyone grabbed
one.

"Hey!" Said Rob. "Why don't we go to a movie?"
They were all shocked at the thought. Stacy threw a
couch pillow at him, missed and knocked over the
antennae that was on the TV. "Hey now, it was just a
suggestion." His brood Cheshire grin alluded mischief.
Beth asked in her best movie star imitation pout,

"Rob, don't you want to be with me alone,
sugar?" She batted her big eyelashes at him. Rob wasn't
exactly ready for that but he took advantage of it.

"Sure I do. My room is back here." He pointed
with a thumb over his shoulder. "Grab your beer and
let's go." While this was going on Stacy was looking at
Sam who was staring at the TV. She picked up a
couch pillow and threw it at him. The pillow hit him
square on the nose.

"Don't you want to be with me Sam?" She asked.
Sam, interrupted now from what he was watching had a
devious look on his face.

"Sure thing babe. I'm starting to get in the
mood." Sam wasn't interested in watching TV any more.

"Well, your mood is going to have to catch up
with mine." She put her arms around Sam and they
started making out. "You're a good kisser Sam." Sam
moved a lock of hair out of his way and started kissing
her neck and nibbling her earlobe. She gave a short
moan in response. He worked his way under her chin
and down to the center of her chest. She said softly,
"Yes." With his index finger, he pulled out the edge of
her tank top and saw the beginnings of her rather
small breast. He wondered if the nipple were dark or

light, large or small. Her nipples pushed out the fabric about an inch. He started to kiss the top of her breast. She moaned another yes and drew her arms tighter around his neck.

Sam lifted the top up over her head and off her arms, exposing the most awesome pair of tiny knockers he had ever seen. He dug his face under both of them reveling in their perfection. His right hand was stuck at the small of her back and the couch so he could only use his left. He began to rub her stomach using just the tips of his fingers. He played around a bit with her belly button piercing. His hand moved to slide in her panties and clasp her perfect ass cheek. Their French kissing was becoming steamy. She was worked up with all the foreplay and began to undo his zipper. She felt his bulge explode from its opening. She rubbed hard at his member until the head protruded from the waistband.

Finally, he had had enough. Lifting her up he wrenched off her shorts and panties. He stood while she worked off his pants and underwear. Her mouth full of his love. They made love twice that night and when Rob and Beth came out the next morning they both started laughing. Sam opened his eyes. He saw he was naked and that Stacy's head was on the floor and the other half of her, also naked, was wrapped up in his legs. Rob and Beth got a kick out of their positions. Sam unwrapped himself from her legs and stood up to put on some clothes. Stacy woke up and began to do the same, though she had an angry look on her face directed at her sister and Rob. Beth returned the stare and said,

"What!" Stacy said nothing and continued putting on her clothes. When they were done Rob asked,

"How about some breakfast?" Stacy spoke up in urgency,

"We're supposed to be on the morning shift at the Four F Club. We start at ten and don't get off until seven tonight. Today is our day off at the factory. Can we meet you guys after work?" Sam knew the boys had a lot to do today so he said,

"If the light's on we're home. If not then we have algorithms to work out and that can take all night. You girls can stop by anytime." The girls agreed and made their way to the front door. They both blew a kiss at the boys and left.
The boys were alone now. Sam felt rumblings in his stomach so he said to Rob,

"Breakfast sounds like a great idea. How was your night? He didn't hear a thing from Rob's room though he wasn't paying that much attention.

"It was awesome," said Rob. "I don't want to go into any details, but that girl can grind on a set of nuts. I barely had to do anything before I was getting off and by the third time sweat was just pouring off my face and into hers. The A/C is not working to great in the back of the house. I put a pillow over her face so she could breathe without getting sweat up her nose. She thought I died because I slept with my eyes open again." They showered, dressed, and left the house. They started driving down Rockville Road east and saw a restaurant that served breakfast. Rob pulled into the lot and parked the car.

"Do you think the girls will be trouble for us?" Rob said with a worried tone.

"Nope," said Sam, "because when we're done here we are going to disappear." They finished breakfast right about the time they were to meet the private investigator and headed over to the meeting place. Mr. Montgomery was already sitting in a booth. The boys walked over and sat on the other side. Montgomery said,

"Hey fellas, I got all the info for you. There are gangs all over the city. The biggest one is over by

Garfield Park. Their headquarters, or at least the house they defend the most, is on Crult Street. They have a lot of members and the boys down at the precinct said if you needed any help to just let them know. I also found out that nobody on the force would get caught down there after dark. Usually there is a killing almost every day down there."

"Wow!" Rob said. "That's a lot of info and we appreciate it." Sam reached into his pocket and took out five twenty dollar bills. Hepaid the man. Montgomery said,

"You know, you should enlist the help of some professionals on this. You could get hurt or even killed. These people don't screw around." They got up to leave and shook the PI's hand in thanks.

"We'll be okay. We've had some training from professionals to ready us for this," said Sam. They left the restaurant. Montgomery waved goodbye as they walked by the window.

"This is great," said Sam. "Now all we have to do is scope out this house of theirs and figure out how we can extract their cash." There was some wood burning going on in Sam's brain. Rob nodded his head in agreement.

"We have machine pistols and the silencers will help for sure.

"Are you sure you're alright with all this? You only shot a couple guys on that last job. We may have to kill everyone in the house and I have to be able to count on you. For me, this is excitement and fun. I almost get a boner off it. I like to figure out how to get away with doing the jobs. Unless we get lucky, the cops will come after us soon. We can always use the money to get out of the states but I want so much money that when we leave I never have to worry about it again." Rob considered everything that Sam had said.

"I don't have a problem with that Sam and you can count on me anytime. I wish I thought of the idea first," said Rob. Sam messed up Rob's hair as if he were a kid and said,

"Let's go see where we can get some ammo." They closed the doors of the car and Sam hit the gas. Sam drove a few miles east heading toward the gang's house. He happened to see a gun shop on the next corner. He pulled a U-turn and drove into the parking lot. They got out and Sam stuck one of the machine pistols in his jacket. They entered the shop.

"Morning fellas how can I help you? My name is Joe." Joe was a short guy in his late forties with a balding head, beady little eyes, and one heavy foreign accent. Even though he was short, he looked like the kind of guy you wouldn't want to meet in a dark alley. The boys looked around the place, which was large and it went straight back a good ways, like a typical store front. Sam walked up to the counter where he thought Joe was standing. He actually found he was a midget sitting on a bar stool.

"Do you know of anyone who can get rounds for certain guns on the slide? Someone whose discretion can be bought with cash? Sam asked.

"Well, what are you guys trying to find?" Joe asked. "You can trust me. I sell ammo to the gangs. Just don't go telling anyone that or those I supply will hunt you down." Rob was playing with a Thompson sub machine gun. "That's a fake," said Joe, "I put that there for show."

"Looked real to me," said Rob. Sam got Joe's attention again by placing the machine pistol on the counter. "We need ammo for this," Sam said.

"Wow!" Said Joe. "I haven't seen one of these in quite a while. Since the last gun show I went to. Good manufacturer. They never jam, ya know. They don't shoot as fast on auto as some of the others, but they'll do in a pinch."

"We also need ammo for a Glock thirty-two," Sam told Joe. Sam had Rob's Glock ready just in case this guy was going to be a problem. He seemed to generally want to help them.

"Common guys let me show you what my other customers don't know about. You know, you're lucky because if anyone else was in here this morning I would have sent you away." He locked the door as he passed it and turned the open sign to closed. He then went to a closet and reached up to grab a hold of a shovel hanging on the wall. He pulled the shovel down along the wall about four inches.

One of the floor to ceiling display cases began to move outward. It was closer to where Rob was and it opened enough for a man to walk behind. The boys walked into the room followed by Joe. The room was about a hundred square feet. The walls were covered in firearms of all kinds, even a fifty caliber. Each wall had from waist level down cabinets filled with drawers. All were labeled showing their contents. There were drawers for special and exotic ammo. Elephant gun ammo, trapper darts, you name it, Joe had it. Joe found the drawer labeled Glock ammo. He rifled through it and produced a box of shells.

"Here you go," Joe said holding up a fifty shot box, "How many of these do you want?" Sam came over and looked at the box. He felt the weight in his hand. Sam took out his Glock and released the safety. He filled the clip, chambered a round, put the gun to Joe's head and blew his brains all over the south wall of the room. Joe fell to the floor twitching for a minute and then stopped. A small pool of blood began to drain from the bullet entry.

"Rob, get his keys and double lock the front door.

Make sure you can't see in anywhere and leave the closed sign alone. Turn out the lights out on your way back. I'm going to see what we can use for tonight's surveillance." Rob left the room. He came back a few minutes later and saw Sam loading shell boxes into a larger box he found.

Rob started to look in drawers on the other side. He found a drawer that had silencers in it. He put them all in Sam's box that was getting a bit heavy. They didn't want to take too much because they only had two hands. It would look suspicious if anyone saw them outside. Sam went up front and saw a Glock in the case. Opening the drawers underneath produced three more Glock thirty-twos. Sam handed them to Rob just as he walked up with the box from the secret room.

"This is a jackpot, Rob. What we're going to do is use untraceable guns. This way we can wear gloves during the robbery and discard the guns we don't want to keep. I almost forgot. If we have the chance to use their weapons let's do it. It will save on our ammo."

"Sounds like a plan, Sam," Rob agreed. It didn't take them long to find the automatics those silencers fit on and all the ammo for them. It was quite a haul. They took two hunting jackets off the rack and put the automatic in the arms and the ammo in the pockets. Sam was going to take Joe's car but decided against it. They left Joe in the secret room and closed the door. Sam left the store and packed the trunk with his part of the haul. He got in, cranked it over, and brought it closer to the entrance. Rob came out arms full and Sam went back for a few more odds and ends. He then took Joe's keys and locked the place up. When Sam got in the car, Rob hit the gas and started back toward trailer.

"Aren't we going to scope out this place tonight, Sam?" Sam turned to Rob,

"Yes, but I forgot we're supposed to meet Raphael

to get our ID's and social security cards. We have to get them before we get out of town and that will in turn happen right after we do the job. We won't be going back to the trailer anymore, Rob."

Chapter Eight

Cob and Dawn came into the forensics area of the building. It was large and many of the rooms had full glass walls. You could watch the scientists as they worked on an object or watch what they produced microscopically on a large overhead screen. A young woman sporting a lab coat came up to them,

"Is there something I can help you with?" In a bright bubbly tone. Cob extended his hand,

"I'm Marshal Barrington and this is Marshal Thorn. We understand your working on the Waveland Ave. cases. We were hoping you could give us some info that would help us find the killer?" She shook their hands with a stronger grip than most females.

"I'm Donna Ford, Chief of Forensics." Ford was a skinny girl who wore big rimmed glasses. She had on a white lab coat and her jet black shoes shined of recent polishing. "You're right about those two cases, everyone you see behind the glass is working on them. We are working as fast as we can. We have to wait for some things such as DNA testing and so forth can take a while. You were told about the casings being a match. We also found a match against the shoe prints at Waveland and the partial found at the Addison killings. We have prints off the kitchen counter from Waveland. The owner is a Rob Bertram who lives in Georgia. We found no other prints except for the victims. I hope this is of some help to you. Oh, I almost forgot, the weapons used were a Glock thirty-two and a Colt M1911 machine pistol. We are still working on many other pieces of evidence though." Cob smiled and said,

"Thank you, Miss Ford. This information is great and we'll do our part to clean this scumbag off the streets. At least we have a name now. Have a nice day." He grabbed Dawn by the arm and they both started walking down the hallway toward the elevator. They both knew they would have to contact the locals up in Georgia to find out about this Rob Bertram guy. They jumped in the car and went back to the downtown office. Once they arrived, Cob took Dawn down the hall about two offices from his and motioned for her to enter.

"Well, what do you think?" He asked. Dawn took a look around the room, which was sparse, not a picture on the walls. There was a phone on the desk and the drawers all worked.

"Is this some kind of test?" A questioning look on her face. "It's an office Cob."
Cob came over and putting his hands on her shoulders said,

"Yes it is just an office, but it's yours." A smile broke from ear to ear on her face and she became excited.

"How did you manage this, you old goat?" She asked. Cob started laughing,

"Well, Danny moved to San Diego. Bill Forman, you remember him from the Ghetto Blocks. He just got promoted and moved upstairs. I asked if a certain partner of mine might be able to have an office near me." Dawn was marveling at her new home in the precinct. No more downstairs with the beat sergeants or fighting for table space in the lunch room. She started thinking about what kind of paintings she would put on the walls. She decided on a beach motif because of the calming affect it had on her. Cob went out the door leaving her to her whims. Down the hall she heard,
"Have fun!"

Cob sat down at his desk. He noticed for the first time a squeak in his chair. He made a mental note to call maintenance. He called the Georgia State Marshals headquarters. He asked if they could check out Rob Bertram and put out an all points bulletin on him. He also asked if they had pictures from any prior arrests and to send what they find down to him. Dawn came to Cob's office and sat down on the rather fluffy couch he had there. Cob used it to catch a few winks when he was doing early morning surveillance. When he finished on the phone, she told him about the beach motif for her office. Cob thought it was a great idea. Too many people were stuffing their offices with awards and diplomas. He told her he talked with Georgia and put out an APB on Bertram and that they would be sending pictures soon he hoped. In the mean time, the killing of the gang leader on Addison has caused an uproar among the gangs in the area. Two attempts on rival gang henchmen had gone on so far and there was general unrest between gangs. Some believed it is a police vigilante trying to wipe them all out. Almost every gang with more than thirty members were tripling their security.

The people in charge of these gangs have gone into hiding thinking the worst. One news report listed the killings as worse than the Saint Valentine's Day Massacre. Another said if you slid a cup across the floor, it would fill with the blood of the dead by the time it got to the other side. Ex-police chiefs and ambitious young reporters were playing out every imaginable scenario on the news. In just a matter of time, the News Reports whipped the city into a frenzy of unstable gang action. Cob knew the answer lied with Bertram. He thought, *why was he there and did he know the victim.* Cob tried to put Bertram in his mind to see what reason he could have for killing that person. Was it money, a move up in the world of gangland? Dawn's cell rang. It was forensics. They said they had found some hair on the clothes of the victim that was not his. Holding the phone four inches from her face Dawn said,

"You told us you didn't find anything on the clothes." The chief of forensics told her that they had not found anything on the shirt. The jeans yielded a different story. Cob leaned back in his chair waiting. Dawn talked for another few minutes and then hung up. "She says they got something off the clothes." Cob sat up straight.

"Are they running DNA yet?" He said to Dawn.

"Yes. It seems that Georgia has sent information over to them from a case ten years ago on this Rob Bertram. Once they work the slides and put together some more history on Bertram they will be able to confirm if Bertram is our man. They transferred me to the front desk who confirmed that the APB is out on Bertram. The Georgia locals talked with Bertram's mother who said he had not been home in a year. She was worried and stated that her son was a good boy on local TV so we have a lost soul here." She stood up from the couch ,put her hands on her waist, and askedCob, "Where would you go if you just killed ten people?"

"Well, I would probably beat it out of town. The question is why kill one guy and then go kill ten

more the next day? We've had the airport on alert and
we have some major road blocks set up in strategic
places. We don't have the manpower to close up a State.
We also don't know what our perp looks like." Just then,
Candice, the floor receptionist, came into Cob's office.
She had a picture of Bertram that was faxed over a few
minutes before. Cob took one look and said,

"My God it's only a kid. He can't be more than
twenty years old. What the hell has caused this kid to
start pulling triggers?" He looked at Dawn for some kind
of response. She just shook her head. "Well Dawn, we
have our picture. The pieces of the puzzle are starting to
come together." Dawn looked at the picture and shook
her head again in disbelief. Cob wanted to go down to
forensics just to make sure they hadn't found anything
else. He offered Dawn dinner at this fancy Sicilian
restaurant he knew of. She refused, saying the food there
was fatty. They made their way down to the car. After
flipping a quarter to see who drove, Dawn punched the
gas and down the street they went.

Chapter Nine

Sam pulled up behind the market. Raphael was waiting. He rolled down his window. Raphael was wearing the same clothes he had on yesterday. He looked Sam in the eye and said,

"Here iz what chew asked for, gringo." Sam took a look at what he paid for. The ID's were perfect along with the social security cards. "Chew got some money for me?" Sam took out his wallet and passed four hundred dollars over to Raphael. He took the money and put it in a roll that could have been the size of Sam's fist. Sam thanked Raphael and told him he would send people around if they needed new identities. Sam rolled the window up as Rob sped away. They made their way to the gang's hood. They didn't go too far into the hood before Sam parked the car on Shelly Street. Shelly had the best access for parking and the quickest way straight out if the boys were being followed. It was also one of the few lighted streets in the hood. They took the Glocks and three of the machine pistols. Rob found a holder for one at Joe's place.

There was an empty three story building across the street from the gang's house. The windows were all broken out and no lights were on in the first two floors. Somebody was living on the third. They worked their way along the opposite side of the street from the house. They were dressed in solid black and wore black ski masks. Sam picked them up when he bought them clothes earlier. The boys blended in with the shadows. When they made it across from the gang house, a car pulled up and three people got out. The boys flattened near the curb, leaning their backs against a car. Three people walked right past them and into the house they were heading for. They laid there for a while. No more movement came from the house they were going to do some recon from. The boys moved like crabs in the night.

They entered the second floor apartment and went to the front room windows. They could see why no one lived here. The floor had a gaping hole right in front of the windows. You could see the rotten boards of the floor below. The boys stuck their heads up over the windowsill. They could see the gang's house well from their position. They saw two guys on each end of a thirty foot long porch. There were two guys in a car out front and the back of the house was lit up pretty well.

"Are you seeing what I am Rob," asked Sam.

"Yeah, I see them, six in all out front. I have an idea, Sam."

"Sure Rob, what is it?" Sam was starting to like the way Rob was making an effort to figure stuff out. Rob moved around the hole to the side where Sam was.

"Well, I think we should sneak down and take out the guys in the car. Their window is open which makes things a bit easier. Then I think we should each take a side of the porch and take out the two there. We don't have the luxury of being expected or having dope and cash to trade." Sam thought about it for a minute. He felt it might just work. The only thing they would have to look out for is someone else approaching and or coming out the front door. Sam lowered his voice,

"So, what do you think is going on in the back yard and how do we deal with it?" Sam asked Rob. Rob took out a pack of smokes and beat it against his index finger. He stuck one in his mouth and lifted his jacket as he lit it. Exhaling a deep breath, he told Sam,

"I'm not sure, Sam. There could be a party going on back there or maybe they cut their coke back there. I think we ought to get this over with and get out of town." Sam sat there thinking about what Rob said. He held up a triumphant finger.

"Okay, look." Said Sam happy with his thoughtful end result. "We need to know what's going on back there and I am going to take a look. If they see me somehow at the front of the house, come and help me. If they don't seem to be bothered by anything then just wait till I return, okay?" Rob nodded his approval and Sam left the room.

Rob began to pay great attention to the front of the gang's house. From his vantage point, he could see Sam work his way among the cars and across the street. A conversation began between the porch and the car on the street. Sam made his move to cross then. He made it into the shadows of bushes that separated the houses. No one saw Sam so he continued toward the back.

There was a path made by small concrete squares that ran back to the fenced yard. Sam could not believe what he saw going on back there. There were people of all classes. Many wore suits. The suits were watching three girls wrestling in a children's pool full of mud. Another crowd was watching a cock fight. There were eighteen people not counting who was inside. Sam made his way back to the apartment and filled Rob in on what he had found. Rob laughed at the thought of three girls wrestling in a mud filled pool. Sam said it was quite common in Kentucky.

Sam shinnied around the hole in the floor and braced himself up against the wall under the window. He started munching on a three musketeers bar. He tossed Rob a box of Cracker Jack. When they were finished, each of them checked their guns. They made sure they had full clips and took all safeties off. Sam brought some oil and lubed up the firing pins on all their guns. He dropped some oil down the barrel of the machine pistols, figuring it may slow them from heating up some.

They made their way out of the apartment and down to the street. Rob scooted over and made sure the car he was behind was even with the car the two guys sat in. Sam joined him a moment later. One of the guys on the porch walked over to the door and opened it. He told the others he was going to take a leak. Sam inched to the rear bumper of the car they were shielded by. He stuck his head up and noticed the guys on the porch were having a conversation. He low trotted across the street to the door of the car and said hi to those inside, getting their attention. He plugged the driver in the neck with his silenced Glock and wasted the other through his chest. Fortunately, their final positions made them look like they were sleeping. Rob showed up about a minute later.

"Okay, let's move to the porch. There's a large tree right in front we should able to hide for a minute. On my count let's go." Sam threw one finger, two fingers, three and they both ran around the car and behind the tree. The three on the porch were still into their conversation. One of them looked down the side of the house. Another heard something and looked straight out from the porch. Now they all were looking out to the front. Sam whispered to Rob,

"I think we should just walk up and shoot them all." Rob nodded his head yes and whispered,

"I'll take the two on the left you take the two on the right." Sam nodded his approval.

The boys walked out at a fast pace and began shooting. The guys on the porch didn't know what to make of these guys all in black. They reached for their guns. Sam sent the closest guy over the porch rail with a shot to the chest. Rob shot his closest guy in the head almost right between the eyes and the second in the neck. The Glocks made only muffled sounds as they dealt death with every pull of the trigger.

Rob unscrewed the light on the porch and threw it on top of the bushes between the houses. They were both standing on either side of the door, pressed up against the siding, waiting. They were waiting for the guy who left to take a leak to return. Suddenly the door opened. Sam starts to shove his Glock in the guys face, but somehow he sees the gun and pushes it out in front of him. Sam pulled the trigger and the bullet went through Rob's jacket, grazing his chest, just below the arm.

Rob winced from the pain and his reaction to it brought his gun hand up. The guy didn't realize there were two people. Rob pumped two slugs through the upper part of his chest. They went right through his heart, killing him instantly. He dropped to the floor. Sam looked into the house and down a long hallway. He wondered for a second why all these old houses had long hallways in the center. Weren't they supposed to open into a living room?

No one was present in the hallway. Sam closed the door. They dragged the body and let it drop off the porch at the side corner of the house. "Are you alright?"

He asked Rob. Rob stuck his hand on the wound and brought out blood. His shirt was getting soaked with blood. Rob looked at Sam and said,

"Why are you always trying to kill me? My shirt is soaked with blood but it doesn't hurt anymore. I can live with it. Let's get this job done." Sam agreed and they retook their positions on either side of the door. Sam gave a cursory glance down both sides of the street. Everything was quiet.

Sam opened the door and went in with Rob close behind. Both guns were chambered and ready. Sam switched to his machine pistol. He opened the first door on the right. It was a bath. They went further down the hallway and saw a six-foot opening on the left. Beads were draped across the opening like some seventies hippie lived there. There were no sounds coming from inside the room. Sam stuck his head in through the beads and saw the room was surrounded with couches. The hallway opened into a kitchen on the left. Sam hugged the left side of the hallway with his back. Just before the kitchen, he motioned for Rob to come close so he could whisper to him. Rob stuck his large ear near Sam's face.

"Listen Rob, when we round this corner, you look to the right and I will take the left." Just then, a guy came out of the pantry holding a jar of pickles. He dropped the jar and went for his gun. The boys were ready and two slugs put him on hold at the pearly gates. Sam came around the corner and saw two guys standing up next to the sink. They were making sandwiches. They went for their guns but Sam wasted them in two spurts of his machine pistol. Rob went to what must have been a back door and stuck his head out. There was a porch but no one was present. He closed the door.

They took the guns from the ones they just killed and went out on the porch. They knelt down in front of a window. They were running out of time. Rob got the idea to run to the front door and lock it. At least they might gain some time to plan if they heard someone banging on the door.

"Okay, the best way to handle this is to make our way to the porch door. It opens inside so we don't need to worry about someone in front of it. We take out the guy standing on the stairs. Then, I walk down the stairs and spray everyone full of lead to my left. You walk behind me. Watch the right side and the front. This should only take a few minutes. Then we shut down the lights."

"No, Sam," Rob snapped. "If we shut down the lights everyone who can see them will know something's up." There didn't seem too much time for talk as the guy outside finished his smoke and opened the door. He stepped right into Rob's Glock. No one saw him fall to the floor. No one heard that now familiar puff puff the Glock made like someone hitting a pillow with a drumstick. They had to make their move.

Rob changed to his machine pistol. Sam began to walk down the stairs. When he got to the bottom, he started spraying the entire back yard with lead. Nothing that moved got away from him. The muffled shots of the silencer sounded like beating eggs in a plastic bowl. Other people trying to get away were tripping over the dead. Sam was dealing death as if the pistol was a sheathe and he was black robed Death himself. The cocks flew out of the pen only to be knocked into the garage wall by stray bullets flying. There was a setup under the porch with tables and a bar. Sam threw lead waist high in slow left to right movements. He was the Maestro of a death orchestra.

People there were crowding themselves into the northeast corner of the fence. Three guys took shots at him but missed. Sam mowed them down with hot lead spraying out the nozzle of his gun. The people just fell on top of each other. The pile was two feet high. Two guys came out of the garage and Rob sprayed them with lead. The impact tossed one back into the garage and the other over a trash can left for the party goers.

Suddenly, Sam was pushed into the grass in front of the stairs. A bullet grazed him in the upper shoulder. Rob turned and sprayed the upper floor window as a bullet just missed his head. The guy was knocked back into the window and the darkness of the room behind. A few people were still moving on the pile Sam made. He walked over and casually shot each in the head with his Glock. He could smell the urine leaking out of the dead bodies. Both the boys were hurting from their wounds. They went back inside the house and locked the back door. Sam took a seat in the kitchen and saw a pail with beer on ice. He opened one and took a long drink.

"Rob," said Sam. A tired look on his face. "We need to tear this place apart and find some cash." Rob ran into the room with all the couches and started looking around. The rug looked a bit out of place like it didn't belong. There was a chair on it. He took the chair off, moved the rug, and found a trap door. He went to Sam who had finished his second bottle,

"Hey Sam I have a trap door over here. Let's check it out," said Rob. Sam got up and followed. He winced from the bullet wound and the movement of his arm. Sam stood in front of the opening with his machine pistol pointing downward while Rob lifted the door. It was black as pitch inside. Rob stuck his hand down along the side and found a switch. When the lights came on they saw a long slender vault with shelving on either side. There were no cases, bags, or boxes, nothing but stacks and stacks of cash on one side. There was about three times as much as the last job.

Rob went upstairs to try to find something to put it all in. He came down later with two suitcases that rolled on wheels. The boys started to pack them full. Rob found a makeshift door on one of the far walls. He didn't know what he would find when he opened the door, but low and behold, there were ten gold bars staring at him. He motioned for Sam to come take a look. When Sam arrived, his eyes grew large and words seemed to be stuck in his throat.

"Holy shit!" He finally exclaimed. "The thing is Rob, we can't carry them all. They weigh way too much and we have to split this place." Sam said. They both stared at the bars. Rob had never seen a gold bar before in real life. They both stuck one in their suitcase Sam yanked on Rob's shirt.

"Let's get the hell out of here." They both dragged their suitcases up the stairs and to the front door. Sam went back and closed the trap door and put the rug back the way it was. He moved the table back into place also. They left a lot of cash back down there. Sam cracked the door open and winced when his shoulder scraped against the door jamb.

No one was outside or on the street. Sam looked at his watch. The job so far had only taken fifteen minutes. They needed to get away. They walked to the end of Crult Street the wheels of the suitcases making a rolling racket. Rob started to have an anxiety attack at being out in the open. They made a left at Shelby Street carrying the suitcase alongside them so as to minimize the noise. It was a great idea to shove the machine pistols in the suitcases also. Sometimes Rob came up with workable ideas. They looked like they were catching a plane, though most of the people in the hood there couldn't afford to ride in one.

Shelby Street was lit up as was expected. No reason the hood would shoot out these lights, after all, the gang members needed to see where they were going. They rolled the suitcases to the car and shoved them in the trunk. When they got inside Sam high-fived Rob, started the car, and slammed on the gas. The car lurched forward on its way to Kentucky.

Chapter Ten

Cob and Dawn arrived at the forensics floor of the county administration building. The building was built in nineteen twenty-seven. It looked every bit like it would fall over any minute. Cob and Dawn were heading for the more stable part of the building. Chief Ford waved from inside her glass office and motioned them to come in,

"Hello Marshals. We have a boatload of evidence for you today. The hair we found had different DNA on it than the victim and it does not match the Bertram suspect. Would you like some coffee? I have medium roast Colombian?" Dawn shook her head no, but Cob said,

"Yes please, I could really use some energy." She got up from her desk and went to the wall unit where the coffee pot found a home. She continued as she poured.

"Cream and sugar, Marshal?" Cob responded

with an affirmative. "My team should have an answer
if the suspect is in any of the files currently in our
database. Let's go take a walk." She walked back and
handed Cob an ornate cup with gold trim. She began to
walk out of the office with Cob and Dawn trailing. They
passed through a section they had not seen before. In
this glass fronted room were massive computers and
reel-to-reel tapes spinning in the back shadows. Six large
screens sat four women and two men. Chief Ford
directed them to the fourth man.

"Have you found anything, Paul?" She asked.
Paul was a lean man. Tall by the way his knees when
sitting were up higher than his waist. Either he liked that
position or his chair wasn't working. He wore black
rimmed glasses and talked with a lisp.

"Yes Chief. The suspect's name is Sam Gamble.
Last known address was in Alabama, Montgomery to be
exact." Cob was pleased with this information. Now he
had two suspects to look for.

"We'll send out an APB with the locals there,"
Cob said. "I doubt he will be anywhere near that
town." Chief Ford and Paul looked at Cob. It appeared as
if Cob was staring right into the wall. Finally, Dawn
asked,

"Are you okay?" He seemed to snap out of it.

"Yes. I'm okay. I just don't think we're going to
find the suspects anywhere they used to live. Probably
not in their own state."

Chief Ford took them to another room. This room
housed the ballistics specialists. They performed the
examination of guns, shells, and trajectories. She turned
to face them both,

"I just wanted to say that these suspects of yours
have killed half the local drug heavy's in town. It is going
to take a long time for them to recover. I would wager
these little gang skirmishes we are seeing now will turn

into full scale war." Cob was looking at the Chief but had other things on his mind.

A calculated grin appeared on Cob's face.

"I think I have a plan," he said. "What if we were to spill the beans on these two as possible suspects with evidence that we are eighty percent sure they did it? Doing this would not only stop the infighting to some extent, but it would cause the gangs to do our work for us. We'll post the pictures of these two and see what happens." Dawn was disturbed by Cob's thinking.

"Cob, If you do that. Then you'll be setting our suspects up to be killed. We are still not positive they actually killed anyone. All we know is that they were there. The gangs won't catch them and turn them in. They will torture and probably just slice their throats. Justice would never be done."

"Well maybe you're right." Cob surrendered to her, "But it sure would be nice to have a thousand other people helping us catch them," said Cob. The Chief picked up where she left off,

"We found the shoe cast taken from Addison Avenue came from a Nike Air Jordan. They are sold all over America and of special interest to the 686 gang here in Chicago." Cob sat down in an old chrome chair by the door.

"So, you are saying now that a gang who wants to take over territory might have started this all? I can't believe that," he scratched the top of his head.   "For one thing, we have two people involved from out of State. Wouldn't the gangs want to take care of it themselves? I mean why hire from outside." The Chief leaned up against the counter Dawn was already occupying.

"No. I am not saying that. It could just be a coincidence. The suspects are wearing a shoe that is popular with gangs and we are not sure that the cast is from one of the suspects. Anyone could have left a sole print in the dirt. A friend who was visiting from the detention center just happened to notice the cast while he was here and gave me the info." She started walking to her office. Cob got up and followed with Dawn trailing. She entered her room, walked around her desk and sat down. Dawn couldn't help but wonder,

"If they did the killing here, why would they go back to where they lived? Unless they didn't think we could pin the killings on them."

"They wouldn't," The Chief said surprised her tone lost its effectiveness. "They would go somewhere else. And if killing ten people didn't bother them then blood lust may have set in. There's no telling where they could go or do." Dawn's cell started to ring. She pulled it out, tapped it, and put it to her ear.

"Yes, yes, what was that? Where exactly is it? Uh huh, yes, on the corner, yes, great, thanks much." She tapped off the phone. "That was a local station. They received a call that people have spotted the subjects all along the Dan Ryan Expressway. Several Gas stations think they saw them. Also a guy who owns a fruit stand just off the expressway says they stopped to buy bananas." Cobb was out of his chair moving to the door with Dawn following.

"Thanks much for your help and the coffee, Chief Ford," he said heading out her office door. "What we need to do now is go talk to some people. Dawn, get on the horn, extend the blocks, and search to the south using the Dan Ryan as a benchmark. Have the local boys check all the hotels a mile on each side of the expressway." Dawn had her phone to her ear and was talking at the same time Cob was. They got to the elevator, through the lobby, and out to the car in just a few minutes. Cob drove this time.

"Where was the first sighting of them?" He asked. Dawn still busy on the phone handed him a paper with the information. "Thanks," said Cob. He started the car and squealed the tires out into traffic.

Cob had two choices to get to the Dan Ryan Expressway. He could go west until he ran into it or he could take either West Cermak Road or Roosevelt Road. His second option would be to go straight on Michigan Avenue, connect with the Stevenson Expressway, and change to the Ryan near State Street. He chose the latter. It was a nice day. Things were looking up in the case, the sun was shining, and they had a lead of sorts. It was windy and the clouds were blowing in off the lake. Traffic was a bitch, especially on Michigan Avenue, but once out of the city proper it was smooth sailing. Once on the Ryan Cob made for the exit of the first person to allegedly see his suspects. He saw the gas station off the side of the road, but saw another not too far down.

"Did they tell you which one it was?" Cob asked Dawn.

"Nope," said Dawn, "just a gas station was all they said. Pull in here and I'll ask the attendant." A few seconds later Dawn came out. "It's not this one. It must be the other across the street," she said. Cob drove off and wormed his way down the street. He parked in one of the front spaces. They both got out. Dawn dodged a little from a car pulling in so fast it almost hit her door. She gave the driver a rather stern look.

They went inside and found Jeremy Jones. Jeremy was a tall medium build young man who worked part time at the station while going to college. He wore preppy clothes. He had blonde hair and had an old fedora on the top of his head. He led Cob and dawn to a back room where they could talk.

"So Jeremy, what can you tell us about this guy?" Cob showed him a picture of Rob.

"Well, he was a little nervous but no more than most people who come here. He bought a lot of Cracker Jack and Three Musketeers' bars. He kept looking around as if he was expecting something to happen. He was wearing a black jacket with a white pin stripe on the sleeves and he seemed to be in a hurry. I noticed him right away because I had just received a fax of the flier out on him." Cob fished through his file.

"Can you tell me if anyone was with him?" He asked.

"Sure. There was a guy who pumped some gas and then sat in the car. The other guy who was in here paid for everything."

"Is there anything else you can tell me about these guys? Like, what kind of car they had or if anyone else was with them?"

"Well, I didn't see anyone else with them. The car was a Monte Carlo. It was an older model I think, but I am not good with car years."

"Thanks much for your help, Jeremy. You can go back to work now," said Cob. He looked at Dawn,

"At least we have the car now and we are sure they are together in this. Have a local cop come here and get their video surveillance tape for the day. They should have it unless they wipe it every twenty-four hours." Dawn got on the phone. They left the station and headed for the Skyway and the next person who saw the suspects.

They were doing sixty mph when a car doing ninety mph rushed by them. It was followed by one of Chicago's own, siren blaring. Cob put his light on the top of the car. He told Dawn to hold on and slammed the gas pedal to the floor. The car jerked forward.

"At least we can give this cop backup," said Cob. "And he's headed in the direction we want to go. Radio in and let them know we are in pursuit also."

Dawn grabbed the radio transmitter and called.

"Marshal 631 in pursuit 10-80 backup local 1306." Her cell started to ring so she answered it while they were flying in and out the center of the freeway. Dawn's shoulders were jerked from left to right. It seemed this guy they were chasing decided to go on the wrong side of the road for a while. She held her phone tight to her ear,

"Yes, where is that?" She began to write directions. "How long ago? Okay we'll be there tomorrow," she said. She watched as cob maneuvered around some construction barrels. He ended up knocking three out of his way.

"Cob, that was Indiana police Chief Harvey Thump. He notified our captain that two events just happened yesterday in Indianapolis. A gun store was broken into and there was a gang murder where twelve people were killed. We might want to break off this engagement and make our way to Indiana," Dawn advised. Cob was keeping a good pace behind the local cop. He noticed a helicopter not far behind in his mirror. The local cop's car blew a tire. He swung around a car that was trying to get out of his way. The cops car flipped onto the side of the road. Cob slammed on the brakes, jerking Dawn almost into the dash. It was a good thing her seat belt held up.

"Get out and make sure that cop is okay. I'll come back and get you on the street side."

Cob hit the gas and screeched the wheels, moving the car into heavy traffic. He noticed the copter keeping straight above the car he wanted. Then the nutjob cut across three lanes of traffic and scooted up the ramp. Cob punched the gas and caught up to him. He nudged the guy's car using a pit maneuver and it worked. The nutjob's car spun and flipped twice, throwing the guy to the grass. He wasn't moving so Cob walked over and cuffed him and also put a tie strap he got from the car around his ankles. After a few minutes the local cops showed up, cut his strap, and let the ambulance guys take a look at him. The locals put him in a cruiser for the ride back to the jailhouse. Cob left to pick up Dawn. She was standing on the curb when Cob pulled up. She got in the car.

"Did you catch the guy?"

"Yeah, I did a pit maneuver and he flipped," Cob said with a smile on his face. "I'm sure he has a pretty big headache right now." They stopped to get some dinner at a diner where there were more trucks than cars. Cob knew there would be good food here. They sat down and placed their order. In a somewhat nonchalant way Cob asked Dawn,

"So, what made you become a Marshal? I mean, it's not a job fit for just anyone and there are little perks."

"Well, my dad was a Marshal in North Dakota. He was on guard duty to the Governor. He got fat working that job. But he always told me, 'if you think you can't do it, try it anyway' and he meant for me to use those words in my everyday life. Boy, oh boy, have there been a lot of things I failed at trying to do but you know I learned about those things and myself during every attempt and I am a better person for it." She poured some cream in her coffee after Cob pretty much dumped the entire sugar bowl in his. He took a sip and said,

"That's a great story. I wish I had one as good as yours, but I started as a beat cop in L.A. and fumbled myself up the ranks. I failed the lieutenant tests and did a few short years with homicide. Then I took a Marshal exam and passed." The waitress returned with their food. Cob continued, "I think after we eat we can get a couple of rooms at the motel across the street. We can take off in the morning for Indianapolis, because the chase is on. That sound good to you?" She was jamming a large fork full of leafy spinach in her mouth as she nodded in the affirmative.

Chapter Eleven

Sam and Rob were moving down highway sixty-five keeping right at the speed limit. Rob was munching on Cracker Jack and Sam was biting chunks off a three musketeers bar. Metallica was playing on the radio. It was a bit cloudy, but they didn't expect rain. The old Monte Carlo Sam bought was running well and the fabric seats were comfortable. They didn't have any trouble paying for gas since money was no longer an issue. This was evident by the twenty ounce porterhouse steak they had had at a Ponderosa. Rob slouched back further in his seat and asked,

"Where we going in Kentucky, Sam?" Sam tossed a candy wrapper out the car window. He turned to Rob and said,

"We're not going to Kentucky. It's too close to where we are now. We have to put some miles behind us. I have a friend in Chattanooga, Tennessee I haven't seen for a while. Actually, he is kind of an Uncle to me. He should be able to put us up for a while so we can get a strategy together for what we will do next. He smokes a lot of dope. If he hasn't killed himself yet we should be well taken care of. He owns a marina at Red Bank. It's just a place for people to dock their boats, but he makes a lot of cash from selling gas. He has a manager that runs the place. I doubt if he set foot in it for years." An idea came to Rob,

"Does he have a boat we can lay low on or should we buy one?" Both Rob and Sam laughed. Sam pulled into a rest area for a bathroom break. Rob went to get some cokes from the machine. When Sam entered the bathroom, he noticed in the mirror that the wad of cloth he had put on his wound was sticking up too much. He thought he would take care of it at the next motel, but then he remembered Ollie had a complete med kit at his house. Ollie was always getting cut up when he worked around the house. Sam came out of the bathroom. Three guys stood a few feet from the door. There was no way around them. They looked like bikers, but none of them were big. Each one did have a weapon. The tallest one in the middle said,

"Just throw down your wallet and you can go on your way." Sam looked this guy in the face and said,

"You don't want to fuck with me, pal." The guy seemed to be a bit intimidated by Sam's courage. The guy asked,

"Oh yeah, what are you gonna do about it?" Sam reached to the small of his back and pulled out his Glock. The next thing Sam heard in near unison was,

"Shit, he's a cop. Get the hell out of here!" They stumbled on the tile entry with their boots which sported horseshoe cleats. They took off toward the parking lot. A minute later he heard squealing tires.

Sam walked out to the parking lot and saw Rob running towards him.

"I ran over when I saw those guys tearing ass across the lot. What went on in there?" Sam adjusted the Glock in the small of his back,

"Well. They wanted to rob me, I guess. At least until I showed them a reason not to." Rob laughed and put an arm around Sam's shoulder as they walked back to the car. It was Rob's turn to drive so Sam got comfortable in the passenger's seat. He drank some of his soda. They both knew that spending too much money in one place would not be a good idea. Also the boys didn't want to be seen by too many people. The boys stopped in Nashville for breakfast and got a room. They decided to get some sleep because it would be party time when they got to Chattanooga. They had just sat down in a booth when a waitress for the truck stop sat down next to Sam. Neither one said anything to the waitress.

"Look," she said. "I don't want to tell you guys what to do. But your pictures are plastered all over the TV. They're saying you're wanted for questioning and that you are suspects in an ongoing murder case about drug gangs. I am okay if you did it because my brother was killed by a gangster. I wanted to warn you before you stayed here very long." They both looked at each other and then at her. Sam put his hand out,

"Thanks a lot, we really appreciate it." They all got out of the booth. The girl went back to her work and the boys beat it out of there quick.

They got back on the road and stopped at Mickey D's for a burger. After they ate, they slept in the car for a few hours at a mall parking lot. Once back on the road, they made it to Chattanooga by nightfall and to Ollie's house by nine that evening. Ollie saw them coming up his private drive and went out to see who it was.

Ollie was a good old southern boy. His granddaddy helped supply ammo to the Smith's during

the Smith/McCoy feuds. His great Uncle made
moonshine until he died when Ollie was little. He liked
to wear farmer jeans and black t-shirts. He was skinny as
a rail and walked with a certain authority. He was a real
doper and smoked only the best Ghanga. Ollie had no
money problems. His family owned half the land along
the shores of a river and his marina was quite large. Sam
remembered him sitting in his four room house screwed
out of his mind most of the time. Sam saw something
quite different about Ollie as they pulled up to the front
of the house. Ollie waved and a smile spread across his
face.

"Dang, is that you Sammy? I declare, it has been
a while since these old eyes got a look at you. How are
you doing Kid?" He asked as Sam got out of the car and
began walking toward Ollie. A smile across his face.

"I'm doing great, Ollie," he gasped as Ollie
grabbed him around the waist and lifted him off the
ground. "Whoa! Man, your squeezing me to death,
dude," Sam almost cried. Ollie looked over at Rob,

"And who do we have here Sammy?" he asked
grabbing Rob's hand while showing his big southern
buck toothed smile.

"My name is Rob." Rob couldn't help but smile.
Ollie's was contagious.

"He's a real good friend Uncle Ollie," said Sam.
"We've been traveling together for a while now." Rob
opened the trunk and took out the suitcases. He gave
one to Sam and stood there in front of Ollie. Ollie got
right up into their faces and said,

"Look boys, your pictures are slapped all over the
TV. The news people are writing about you, and there is
even a bounty on your heads for forty thousand each."
He backed off a bit then. "Now, I want you to know that
you're safe here and personally I think you should take a
break, rest, relax. I have a thirty-three foot Bayliner over

on Lake Guntersville that I use to take women out on. We can go live there for a few weeks. Maybe this hunt will blow over but I doubt it, now that they know it was you." Rob and Sam stared at Ollie. It was kind of amazing they made it on the daily news.

"How are we going to get to the boat without being seen, Ollie?" Sam asked. Ollie snapped his fingers in the air.

"That's not a problem boy," Ollie replied. "I have a limo with blacked out windows and a private dock. Common inside, have some grub, and tell me about your exploits. To be honest, it's been pretty damn boring around here. It would be nice to chat with somebody different."

The boys dragged the suitcases inside the house. This was not the house Sam remembered. He wondered what happened to the old one. This one was more like a mansion. Giant staircases led up both sides of the entryway. There was an eight-foot round table in the center with a giant bouquet of flowers in the center. The marble floors were laid out in a complex geometric pattern.

As they walked further in Sam, who spent time on a trim crew in Alabama, was amazed at how ornate the dental crown moldings looked. He also noted the painted medallions of the light fixtures. The dining room was twice as large as any he had seen before. It had niches with small Greek like statues in each one. They went into what the boys thought was a living room. It was actually a sitting room complete with wet bar. A few animals unlucky enough to walk in front of Ollie's shotgun lined the walls. Sam wondered how many people have a badger mounted so it looked like it was crawling up the wall. It was all a bit much for Sam to take in.

"Ollie, this is a mansion. What happened to the other house?" Sam asked. Ollie turned to Sam,

"Oh, that old thing," he said with a laugh. "I had it ripped down early last year just after you left. It was an eyesore. Matter of fact the crew just finished the west wing of the new house last month. It has an indoor swimming pool with rock grotto, waterfall and slide for the kids. Some of the girls I see have children," Ollie explained. Just then, one of the blackest women Rob had ever seen came into the room.

"Will you be having dinner this evening, sir?" She asked. Ollie turned toward the woman and then back at the boys.

"Boys," Ollie began. "This here is Mable. She is chief cook and bottle washer around here. She tells everyone what to do so they stay out of my hair. She runs the whole house. In fact, she makes one hell of a Dagwood sandwich. Would you boys care for something to eat?" Both Rob and Sam looked at each other then they both agreed they would like the Dagwood. Mable left the room.

Ollie took the boys to a secret room that was just beyond a door in the hallway. Once inside, they found a twelve by twelve room with one whole wall covered up from waist high in TV monitors. A plush leather chair stood in the center surrounded by monitors, banks of lights, and microphones. It looked like the bridge of Star Trek's Enterprise. Ollie chuckled,

"Yes sir, this here is my communications center. I can see people coming from the start of my private road. I can see people two miles out on my property. I have cameras and infrared night vision spread out all over my property. My property extends from Guntersville lake all the way here to RedBank. Every window in the house has one inch thick plastic resin in front of one inch thick Kevlar layered glass so it is almost impenetrable. Even a mortar round only does minimal damage. The house is made of two foot thick concrete walls, roof, everything. The engineers say it will withstand a category six hurricane if we had those up here. Anyway, the little tornadoes we have had just strolled by the windows while we watch. Sounds like a swarm of locusts hitting the glass. They do tear up my trees and uproot most of the plants though. Wait till you see this."

Ollie walked them down a flight of stairs. He stood before a huge stainless steel bank vault. It stood about nine feet round and looked complicated.

"It only works off the tones of my voice. He demonstrated, "Molly Hatchet." The boys could hear gears working and metal sliding into place and then the door opened. Beyond the door was a room you could barely see the end of. It had to be forty feet wide and was filled with opulent furniture from around the world. There was a hot tub in a glass surround that would sit at least ten people.

"What is this place, Ollie?" Sam asked. Ollie walked around with his hands in the air,

"This, my friends, is a fallout shelter. It is completely self sufficient. You can live in here with the door closed for ten years without needing anything. I have canned food of all kinds, water from a deep well just below the center of this room, and the swimming pool water can be filtered and used also. There are vats that breed salmon, lobster, and trout. Also a hybrid plant operation that doesn't need the sun to grow tomatoes, greens, and potatoes. I have the local college kids come down here to study how this eco friendly home away from home works. I have heard they have adapted the technology elsewhere."

"The walls, ceilings, and floors are six feet thick. This place can withstand a nuclear blast three miles away. A direct hit is questionable. We have been arguing whether it would survive for the last four months. It cost me next to nothing since I bought the concrete company. We haven't been able to do many other jobs because my house took precedence." Sam and Rob couldn't believe what they were seeing. They walked around for ten minutes taking it all in. Just then, Mable came in with a platter full of sandwiches.

"Your dinner, sir," She said. They thanked Mable while she was on her way out of the room. They moved back into the main house. Rob carried the platter. Just for fun Rob said, "Molly Hatchet," but nothing happened. Ollie laughed,

"It only works to the specific pitch sounds of my voice. Took the tech guys three months to make that happen. You could make a recording of my voice and it still wouldn't open. It can tell between a copy and me." Rob sat down and put a sandwich in front of him, grabbed it with both hands, and sunk his front teeth into it.

"Ummmm umm," He said eyes rolling back in his head. He said something else, but it wasn't understandable. Sam grabbed a sandwich, but took smaller bites. He wasn't hungry and he figured Rob would eat what he didn't. Rob was a human garbage disposal.

After dinner, they sat in the badger room. That was the name Rob had given the sitting room. Ollie brought out a bottle of Dom Perignon and poured everyone a glass.

"Let's celebrate us getting together. A toast to your endeavors, may they be as wide as they are deep," Ollie said with a wide smile. He set his glass down on the table. He then sat on the table in front of them.

"Look boys, I don't know what you call doing what you do and I don't care. Sammy, you're a young kid moving up in the world, but let me say that with all this money and stuff, I am bored. I went hang gliding the other day and balloon riding the day before. I jumped out of a helicopter onto Big Sky Mountain and skied down the bowl. I did that in the Alps too but I don't like powdered snow as much. I'm telling you I am bored stiff. Three weeks ago, I went to a farm where you could hunt animals down in Florida. They asked me what I wanted to hunt and I said wild boar. They told me how dangerous they can be. That I might find one running at me at fifteen miles an hour and how those tucks can rip your skin right off the bone. I said I didn't care and signed an agreement. I need some action. So, I want in with you boys." Sam and Rob looked at each other and then back at Ollie. Sam took a drink before clearing his throat to speak,

"Ollie, I'll tell you what happened. We were doing a job for Felix."

"Oh? Your father's brother."

"Yes. A gangster stole some cocaine and cash from his clubhouse. We were sent to get the stuff back and kill this guy. Rob and I never killed anyone before, I mean, you know me, I was never a killer." He turned to Rob, "Rob, please go get one of the suitcases." Rob got up and left the room. "After we did that job we were sitting on sixty grand cash and I wanted more. It felt good to kill that scum. Then it hit me. Why not go after a bunch of drug lords and gangsters and put some of them out of business? Rob and I could score big and settle down somewhere special." Rob returned with the suitcase. "Look here, Ollie," Sam continued. Sam unzipped the suitcase. Ollie could see the machine pistol, stacks of cash and the bar of gold.

"How much is in that case?" Ollie asked.

"About five hundred thousand, give or take a few broken packs. There's another suitcase just like it." Sam pointed in the direction of the room.

"You mean to tell me you made one million dollars just by killing some scum?" Ollie couldn't believe it. Sam was nodding his head yes. Rob had a smile a mile wide on his face.

"But Ollie," Sam said, "you have to understand something. Rob and I plan what we are going to do. We even hired a private investigator to gather information. So a lot of planning happens. Even with planning in place, Rob was grazed by a bullet in the left shoulder and I was hit in my right shoulder. Oh, and a million dollars was all we could carry. We must have left five million more just because we couldn't find anything to carry it in. If you decide you want to play for keeps with us, you have to understand you may not be coming back here. Life as you know it will be gone." Ollie got up from the table and moved to the couch. He was thinking real hard about what Sam had to say. Finally. After pulling on his hair a bit. He turned to the boys and said with a smile on his face,

"You know, if it's your time to go then it is. I am so excited, I can't wait to get started. We'll have everything I have at our disposal. In fact, I'll make a call right now. I'll get some information about local drug lords or gangs working in Chattanooga. I'll be back in a minute."

Rob sat up straighter and finished Sam's half of sandwich.

"Damn Rob, don't you get enough to eat?" Sam asked. They hung around and drank some more champagne. Finally Ollie returned,

"Okay boys, I got the ball rolling. Let's get some sleep. I'll have the information we need late in the morning. I also talked with a friend of mine. You have some marshals chasing you. Tomorrow they will be on their way to Indianapolis. When we get the info you boys can tell me what we have to do next." Sam walked over to Ollie and stuck out his hand,

"Glad to have you on board, Ollie. Rob, let's get some sleep." Just then, three girls came into the room. Ollie got up off the couch.

"Boys, these here girls are Sugar, Velvet, and Goldie. I thought you might like a swim and a dip in the hot tub before you retired for the night. They were coming over anyway," Ollie said. Ollie didn't tell the boys that coming over meant from one wing of the house to the other. Without hesitation, Rob held out his arm for Velvet. She was a six foot tall brown haired woman wearing a strapless bikini. She was tanned and her toenails were impeccably finished.

Sam held his arm out for Goldie. She had a bath robe on that said Palmer House Chicago on it. She was shorter than Velvet and was a bit more full breasted. Her bikini sported little red hearts on a black background. Ollie took hold of Sugar (which was his favorite) and began telling her what a nice smile she had. They all played in the pool room for about an hour. Goldie ended up in her birthday suit. No one seemed to mind except that Rob at times looked like he couldn't make up his mind. Sam mentioned they could trade, but then Rob thought better of it. They spent thirty minutes in the hot tub, toweled off and went to bed.

The next morning was a bit hectic. Ollie was running around waking everyone up and chasing the girls toward the west wing. The boys finally found out the west wing housed the girls' living quarters. Mable set out breakfast for the three of them in the dining room - blueberry pancakes hot off the griddle, rye toast, lox, bagels and pouched eggs. Rob was dressed and sat at the end of the table. Sam sat at the other end about ten feet away and Ollie sat in the middle with his head down studying that day's paper. The house phone sat next to his right arm and there were maps laid out about two feet to each side of him. Ollie swore because he had spilled coffee on one of the maps. Sam was lapping up some syrup from the second order of blueberry pancakes,

"What the hell is going on Ollie?" Sam asked. "You're like a general making a battle plan." Ollie picked up the phone, thought better of it and said to Sam,

"Not a battle plan. More like an information plan. You have to have info if you're going to do something right. Eat your breakfast." Rob was working on his second helping of large German sausage links.

"So Ollie," Rob inquired. "do you have any guns around here?" Ollie looked up from his papers a big smile on his face. He motioned for Rob to come with him. As they rounded the table Sam got up also. He opened the door to the left of the badger room and walked in. Rob and Sam followed. It was quite dark for a moment and then blazing bright lights came on. What they saw was amazing.

There were M-16's, a bazooka, three Thompson machine guns, just on one wall. The other wall had all manner of hand guns. A Colt 45, Police Special, four different types of Glocks. The mother of them all were the rocket launchers. "For ground to air problems. You understand," said Ollie. There was also a fifty caliber machine gun three legs held up the monster in one corner. The place was jammed with enough ammo and silencers to start a small war. Then there was a Ballisti-Cast II bullet maker. The room reminded Sam of the gun shop owner in Indianapolis. He felt sorry for the guy. He took his life for no real reason other than to steal whatever he wanted. Ollie was watching the boys look the room over.

"Is that enough guns for you, Rob?" Ollie asked. Rob was running his hand down the Ballisti-Cast II's side.

"Yes, Ollie," A broad grin across his face, "I think you answered my question just fine." The boys and Ollie went back to finish breakfast. Ollie stuffed and English muffin in his mouth and continued to rattle around the maps he was working with. The phone rang and he picked it up. Mumbling a few words to himself, he put the receiver down and went back to coating another muffin with Marmalade.

Chapter Twelve

Cob and Dawn woke up early, each in their respective rooms, where they slept well. They had about four hours of traveling left to do before arriving in Indianapolis. They had been talking over breakfast about the reasons behind these killings. Dawn thought Rob started by killing the guy near the bowling alley. Then found he was in trouble, and called in Sam for help.

Cob questioned why he had to kill the first guy. He didn't take any money out of his wallet. Even though the door was off the hinges this guy had to know who was in the house. Dawn felt there was no particular reason for the killings. She told Cob so far as anyone knows, they were a team that wanted to take out gangsters and drug lords. Cob told her it just didn't make sense. The print & polish team couldn't find any cash or drugs on the premises. Unless they were paid by a top drug lord to open up some territory. Or maybe to fix a supply chain? Cob couldn't put two and two together just yet. The problem with the whole thing was the kid's records. They were not killers. They had no priors for weapons. They had no military training. Cob needed more information.

They arrived late afternoon in Indianapolis. The sun was just sliding behind the horizon. Traffic was picking up for dinner. They met with Chief Thumps in his office.

"Hello Marshals', I'm glad you made it down here. We had forensics taken both scenes apart while we were waiting for you. We wouldn't have associated the gun shop owner until his wife called in and we went to check it out. You should see the owner's secret room. Anyway. His wife was so mad because she thought the gang he was selling to might have killed him off just to get his stuff. There wasn't much missing. There were a couple of jackets, some boxes of shells and a few other things. There were no prints and they found his car right outside like it had been there all day. Funny thing is one of the people who got killed at the house was an assistant district attorney. When that got out on TV the DA was pretty pissed." Cob had to ask a loaded question.

"What was the assistant district attorney doing in a dope dealer's house?" The chief sat down in a chair.

"I don't know," said the chief with some regret, "but you can bet with this being an election year somebody is going to find some wrong doing here. There was a girl's mud wrestling match going on in the yard. You'll see when we get there. It won't take long." The chief got up and walked out of the office down the stairs to the car. Cob and Dawn trailing. The chief gave orders to a view plain clothes detectives as they walked. He drove a black Crown Victoria. It was a typical administration model. It had light brown leather seats with a bored and stroked four hundred cubic inch engine under the hood and solid rubber tires. The laptop was mounted just to the right of the steering wheel and the shot gun just to the right of the computer. It had a roll cage and bullet proof windows, along with a hands free microphone for the radio.

Cob whispered to Dawn to remind him to ask for one like that when they got back to Chicago. He doubted he would get it, but then he thought, he was due for a raise. They drove out to the gun owner's shop. Cob noticed the neighborhood was lower middle class. The street were dirty with unclean gutters and graffiti on building walls. They got out of the car and Cob immediately looked over the parking lot. He saw some tracks in the mud. One was a sneaker.

"Hey chief," said Cob, "Did the forensics people make a cast of any of these?" The chief took a look at what Cob was pointing at,

"I don't think so," said the chief. "I'll call and find out. Oh, they call themselves CSI's down here." Cob put a hand to his chin and said,

"CSI's, huh. I heard of those before.
They're supposed to be the ones who have no experience in the field but went to college. So now they can tell us what we already know, am I right?" The chief put his hands on his hips and said,

"Down here Marshal, we have found that these CSI people do know what they're looking for. They have the equipment to find it also." They went in through the door. Cobb said to Dawn,

"How about you take a good look out here while take a look in the secret room. Let's see what they're all talking about." She tapped him on the shoulder and whispered in his ear,

"Sure thing. Maybe I'll find some hairs from the killer with my x-ray eyes." Cob snorted a laugh. The door to the secret room was already open but Cob was interested in the means used to open it. Cob found that you couldn't just pick the shovel up to close the door. It had to happen by doing something either inside or outside the room. He went into the room.

"Nice room here. Wish I had one of these." The chief was looking at the guns on the wall.

"If you did," he said with a slight smirk on his face. "You'd be arrested and dragged out with the trash. Just about everything in here is illegal. This guy who owned the place used to come down to the firing range once a month. He has one downstairs but I guess he liked the company." Cob picked up a couple of the handguns,

"Any of these been fired recently?" He asked to no one in particular.

"No. The CSI folk went through here with a fine tooth comb. After all, you gave them the whole night to investigate. They did the best job we've seen yet," said the chief.

"So when did they wrap it all up?"

"Well, I'd say about two hours ago." The chief sat on a stool that was in the corner. "We don't know what they found yet. It may take a day or so, but they're on it. The CSI crew like to lock themselves up in their little world and won't come out until they have reason to." He walked over to the door and saw Dawn on a ladder. "Anything I can do to help you there marshal?" He asked. Dawn was going through some boxes on top of a cabinet.

"Nope." Dawn said turning to look at the chief. "I'm just taking some mental notes. There's a gun up here, but it has so much dust on it. I doubt its been taken down in the last century." She grabbed the gun while balancing on the rickety wooden ladder. She handed it to the chief and he looked it over.   "Hmmmm," he said. "It doesn't have a serial number. I'll have ballistics check it out for priors." Just then, Cob said in a dry unamused tone,

"You mean CSI folks don't you?" The chief gave a little chuckle. Cob moved out of the secret room and went to look at the front. He fumbled around in the drawers under the counter by the cash register.

"Has anyone checked this guy's books to see if he is missing any inventory? Cob asked.

"We have a man who took count of everything in here," said the chief. "Took him most of the night. He took all the record books and receipts but to be honest, it could take weeks to find out." Dawn came out of the secret room.

"Well Dawn, what else do you have? Cob asked. Dawn went behind the counter.

"Cob, I'm afraid I don't have much. There were some records on top of that cabinet over there and a gun no one saw. The records appear to be IRS tax records and his two week wait sheets were all alphabetized. I checked the register earlier. It has about three hundred dollars in it, which is about normal for a business at start of day. When I called the people doing the inventory only two pair of jackets seemed to be missing." Cob slapped the counter.

"Then if these guys are not stealing money, what are they trying to accomplish? We can't tell if they took anything from the secret room because nothing in there was inventoried. I'll bet they don't even find where anything that is in there has a receipt of purchase. It would appear that all they want to do is kill people. That does not correspond with their records, and neither have any military experience. It just doesn't add up." He walked out the door. Dawn and the chief were close behind. Cob took a look at the building and the surrounding area.

"Are there any street cameras around here that might have picked up the suspects, chief? The chief took a look himself.

"I don't think so," replied the Chief. "There is one down on the next intersection. I know the hobby shop owner has one out front, but his faces the front of his building." Cob was getting a bit gnarly dealing with this situation. It seemed every step forward sent him another step back. Cob thought finding the reason behind these killings would be a difficult problem to solve. *They seem so random, so imperfect, so....*

"Let's get over to the other crime scene. I don't think there is anything else to find here," he said. They got in the car and Thumps hit the gas. "How far away is the scene? Cob asked.

"It's a good ten minutes," the chief replied. Cob thought that maybe these kids are not doing things in a random matter. There may be a method to their madness. He turned to Dawn and said,

"Dawn. I would like you to focus on everything we know. Instead of looking for something that can tell us why they are they killing people. Look for a pattern of some kind. Look for something that can tie all the scenes together that makes sense and let me know what you come up with later." Dawn was receptive to this idea. She was getting tired of going over the same things and getting nowhere. A new way to try to identify a purpose was actually welcomed.

"Sure thing, Cob. I'll let you know," she said. She ran back over each scene in her mind trying to figure out a connection and then she had an idea. So far, she thought, the only relationship was gang and drug related. It appeared that they would just walk in and kill. There had to be another reason that they would risk their lives. She thought for a while more as the car passed house after house. The shiny white picket fences blurred for only a moment. She saw that a passageway that ran in between the homes connected the houses to their yards. Many people had nothing to hide or no reason to hide behind a fence.

"Cob, I think I have it." She said.

"Let's hear it," said Cob in response.

"Well. I think we're missing something. We need to get the boys back to Addison Avenue and rip that place apart. We need to look for something we missed before, the dope or cash. We know that the gangs deal in drugs, money laundering, and such. In each case, nobody found anything on the premises. These kids, I do not believe, are on a vigilante bent, I think there is real purpose to what they are doing. The connection being people who engage in criminal activities. I think by ripping the place apart we may find what we are looking for." Cob was glad to have a partner like Dawn. She thought quickly on her feet. What she just said made a lot of sense. They didn't find any stash of drugs and there were no piles of money. A little coke on the table and a few joints were all that was in the house.

"Dawn I think you hit on something," Cob agreed. He rifled through the junk in his pocket and pulled out his phone dialing quickly with his index finger.

"Hello. This is Cob. Put the captain on the line, please. Thank you. Is that you cap? I can barely hear you. Cap, Dawn had an epiphany, we need to send some locals back to Addison and get them to rip the place up. We're looking for secret passages, loose boards in the floor. Something big enough to hide a truck load of cash and drugs. There has to be something there that these kids want and we have to find out what it is. Yes. Give me a call when you find something. I am sure it's there. Thanks." Cob clicked off his phone. "That was a great idea, Dawn I am sure it will yield some good information, if not break this case open. If nothing else, the locals are getting a bit fat, a little hard labor will do them some good." Dawn laughed and even the chief chuckled. Dawn knew he was right. The local cops have been in too many doughnut shops for the free coffee.

They pulled outside scene four. The neighborhood was nothing to write home to mom about. Dawn actually felt sorry for the good people who had to live in this cesspool. It was quite a diverse population. These same people were standing outside the yellow taped off area. The print and polishers had just left. Getting out of the car, she noticed three covered bodies and a cloth over the top and side window of a car.

As they walked up the stairs, Cob tried to imagine how it all went down. It was so open he couldn't get a handle on how they snuck up on them. To make this work, he thought, there would have to be more than two of them or they just walked up shooting. The driver of the car took one in the neck and the passenger caught one in the chest. How did the neighborhood not hear the shots? The locals said there were no calls called in. Cob continued putting the scene together in his mind. The kids approached from the driver's side so as not to alarm those on the porch. But only two of the porch guys had their weapons out. They went inside, walked down the hallway and stopped to look in the couch room. Then they went to the kitchen where three more bodies lay on the floor. One looked like he was coming out of the pantry when he took a slug in the left side of his chest that punctured his heart. It looked like the bullet didn't go all the way through him. No splatter marks on the wall. Judging by the splatter of blood on the cabinets and sink, the kids just sprayed bullets across the room.

Walking out to the porch, they saw little evidence of a struggle. Another stiff body was found laying face down, ass in the air after rigor mortise finally set in. Cob could see bodies laying in the yard. The carnage was evident mostly under the porch and in the corner of the fenced in yard. Almost like an execution took place here. The sunken tables were turned over toward the corner of the fence. That meant everyone ran in that direction to get away from the hot lead flying. The dead lay on top of one another. It was a truly gruesome scene, as if someone were shuffling a deck of human death cards.

Cob and the chief were walking behind the cock fight area. They noticed all the lighting and the two dead by the garage door. Cob wondered if there was this much lighting, why no one saw this go down. When he asked the chief about this, he found that the people who owned this house were dead. They also owned the houses to either side and across the reclamation ditch. He was also informed that people around this area did not snitch. The chief said it wasn't healthy. Cob was beginning to get miffed over these kids. Then Cob's phone rang.

"Yes. They were? Is that good news or what? You did. How much was it? Five million, you have got to be kidding me. It was right there in front of everyone and we walked right by it. Thanks." He put his phone back in his pocket and turned to Dawn after she asked,

"Well?"

"That was the captain over at Addison Avenue," said Cob beaming with pleasure. "They started moving furniture around and they found a movable wall. Behind the wall they found guns, ammo, stacks of cash, and about five million in cocaine. Oh, I forgot. When the locals arrived, there were a few gangsters inside that didn't want to give up the ship yet so they sent them down to Davy Jones just like the commanders of ships in the old days. What this means is that there must be something here. Let's rip this place apart. Tell the coroner that he can take the bodies as long as CSI is through with them. Get us some locals in there to help, okay?" The chief was already on the phone to his precinct.

"In the process, marshal." He said. They began to move furniture around inside the house. Dawn took one end of the couch room and Cob took the other. There were officers moving things around in the yard and checking out the garage. They picked up garbage cans and pushed over a kids swimming pool and stuck a shovel in the grass every ten inches. Finally, Dawn moved the chair by the six-foot entry and lifted up the carpet.

"Bingo!" She yelled and Cob came right over. They pulled their police special thirty-eight caliber handguns. Dawn braced herself for action as Cob went to lift the doorway. Two other locals who heard her stood behind her for extra firepower. Cob whipped the door open. Nothing happened. It was black as pitch down there. She turned back to the locals and instructed, "Hold your position." She then went and reached down on the left side finding a switch and turned it on. Cob, gun at the ready, walked down the stairs. He walked all the way back and then came forward a few steps. "Clear," was all Cob said. Everyone put their weapons away and Dawn joined him down in the cellar. The chief came and waited outside.

"Look at all this money and dope. It's like being in a bank vault. If this is all here and they left a lot at Addison Avenue then we're back to square one on their reasoning. Unless...," Dawn stopped in mid thought. Cob thought some more while he fished through the stacks of cash and dope packs the size of Kleenex boxes. Dawn couldn't believe what she was seeing.

"Cob, stop that!" She yelled. "The print and polishers haven't been down here yet." Cob stopped immediately and apologized. He wanted to see how deep they went. Everything was stacked so nice and neat. She thought there have to be women working in the gangs. The chief walked down a few stairs to see for himself.

"Man, you found the mother lode. How much do you recon is in here?" Cob could only guess, but Dawn burst out saying,

"Well. There are one hundred and fifty boxes of dope and two hundred and fifty stacks of cash. If we have one hundred and fifty keys of cocaine. The street value would be about two point seven million dollars at eighteen thousand each. The stacks of cash, two hundred and fifty in all at four thousand each, equal one million dollars worth. The question is, with all this money and dope here, what did the kids want bad enough to kill everyone for?" Dawn's breakdown grabbed Cob's attention. He was listening intently,

"So we're back to square one then," said Cob. They left the room and called for the CSI crew to come back. When CSI was done, the locals packed it all up for the evidence room. Cob put a hand on Dawn's shoulder and said,

"Dawn. Get on the phone to find out where all the local gangs and drug lords are. Get me four States worth of info. Get somebody to call every narcotics section of every district. Find out where the dope goes after it hits Miami. There is no reason to think they have gone back up north so let's concentrate down here. I want a list as soon as we can get it." He looked at Chief Thumps. "Is there a place where we can set up some maps of these areas? I want to coordinate the information Dawn is putting together." The chief was holding two stacks of cash and promptly put them down.

"This is going hurt this gang." The Chief said, "Of course, marshal. We have a large conference room down at the precinct that we don't use. Unless it's somebody's birthday. It has phones and a video machine with internet." They all left the work to the locals since the

CSI crew just walked in. They hung around the site for a few minutes more. Cob instructed the CSI to look for specifics but was told by CSI that was old school and there were better ways to obtain that information from a site. CSI really ruffled Cob's feathers this time. It made him feel his age. They got back into the car, slammed on the gas, and headed for the precinct.

Chapter Thirteen

Mable came in and cleaned the plates away for everyone. Ollie told her that he and the boys were not to be disturbed. While the boys sat in full bellied contentment. Ollie was receiving many calls on the phone he placed at the table. He started placing maps all along the inner part of the table and had to move a large flowered vase to make room. Sam and Rob moved their chairs closer to the center.

"Just what are you doing, Ollie?" Sam asked. Ollie moved a few papers he had been writing on out in front of him. His arms stretched out with a satisfied look on his face.

"Well, Sam. I've just finished correlating the information I have been receiving for the last fifteen minutes. This paper here shows me the location of all the major gang headquarters. This paper over here shows me where the major drug cartel people live. This other paper here shows who carries the most cash influence in

the city. On this map are marked all the places with a dollar amount, guestimated of
course. What we have are the Del Vega Cartel about fifteen miles to our south. My inside sources have told me that they hold up to ten million dollars in paper cash stored in the basement. Also, an untold number of keys of cocaine. Over here about twenty miles southwest, we have the Los Caballos gang, who run drugs all over the State. The Del Vega's, over here, sell to the upper crust. Los Caballos sell all day long at two hundred locations. They bring all the money in every Friday afternoon. They bring in up to five million dollars a week."

Sam leaned over the table and asked,

"What are these dots for?" Ollie pulled the map closer to him and said,

"These are the small fry. They have only a few million and deal in areas that are well out of the territory of the other two." Sam thought for a second. He liked the idea of an easier target. The others have too much protection most likely. He was thinking that with Ollie they could take this a bit further, but was it worth the risk? Sam looked at Ollie and said,

"Look, Uncle. We want to steal money from the gangs, but we don't want to get killed. I think it might be better if we target smaller people. The larger, more sophisticated, gangs will have more protection that we would have to overcome. We need to stay alive and finish the job. You said we had a boat we could live on for a while. How about we go knock off a smaller gang and go stay on the boat." Ollie pushed his chair back from the table.

"Okay boys," Ollie said grimly, "you said you were going to quit when you get enough money. Why not go for the big guys and get your money? If you keep doing the little guys, every job means exposure and the chance to get caught or killed. You have me now boys, and that means everything at my disposal. I also have people. We have three panel trucks driven by people who know what's going on and have been paid in advance. They will drive to wherever we are, take the money and leave. They'll meet with us later at an established rendezvous. All we have to do is show them where the money is. They get a considerable bonus for doing the work.

Now, as far as not being killed, I have an answer for that to, at least to some extent. I have hired four ex-military sharp shooters. They will take positions in the front and back of wherever we decide to go. They have silenced weapons and will take care of any sentries. They may be able to help on the inside if they can see a problem. We will also have communication rigs in our ears so we can keep in touch with each other. The yellow stripe on the front & back of our jet-black uniforms will distinguish us from the gang. The snipers have been told they are a part of an elite super secret government group. These guys are hot to get the job done and will follow our commands to the letter. What do you say now? Do we go for the small fry. Or do we plan to get rid of some scum and make a hell of a profit?"

Both Rob and Sam showed wider eyes than could be expected of young people showing amazement. Sam had no retort or excuse not to make use of what was just described to him. It kind of gave him a rush. Rob too was amazed by everything he had heard that was at their disposal provided by Ollie. Rob thought to himself, man, this guy is gung-ho to get involved. Sam finally said,

"Well, Ollie. When you put it like that it seems the small fry's are not worth our effort but I have one question. I want to do Atlanta and Miami. Then I want to beat it overseas to some Japanese island where I can live out the rest of my days in luxury and discretion. I am sure Rob would like to do the same somewhere. Are you willing to help us achieve all that? You're already wealthy as hell, what could doing this actually provide for you?" Ollie had a huge smile on his face.

"Sammy boy, as I said earlier, I just want to be part of something. With my money, I can do many things, but once you have done them, they're finished. It has been like smoking a huge joint. You get high and everything is great. Then you start to come down, get hungry, and feel like shit. Well, I am past getting hungry and I feel like shit now, so I need some action. I need real, unforgiving action. I need the kind of action that scares the fuck out of you. I know I could get shot or killed in spite of the measures I will take but it's worth it to me because I want to feel alive. I want the big chance. I want to roll the dice and hope I don't crap out. At least we have some extra help trying to make this dream of yours a reality." The boy's both shook their heads in the affirmative.

"Okay, Ollie," conceded Sam, "let's get this plan on the road." They sat around for the next two hours arguing over which place to hit. Ollie was finally agreeable to robbing the Los Caballos gang. This was only because he realized what Rob and Sam have been saying for the past hour was true. These gangs and drug lords think that bodies surrounding a house are a good line for defense. Ollie still thought that trying to hit a mansion would offer better advantages. They might be able to pick off the guards one at a time without anyone around noticing. Ollie did agree that the drug lords might have earpieces and good communication. The gang wouldn't think of it. In the end Sam insisted,

"It's settled then. We go for the Los Caballos gang and hope for the best. The way our country is run, you would think the whole of Congress and the House are on crack cocaine. It has always been big business people looking for another notch in their gun. You never see a middle class person running for office. When we're done we can see if a small town in Italy needs a Mayor."

That said, Ollie began to write down their steps to victory. They now knew two things. One was that the trucks would be ready to go in, get the cash, and split. They found out later that Ollie had an extra truck to grab all the coke. They also knew that the snipers would put themselves in advantageous positions. They will arrive and leave on their own.

Ollie set the job for today. The snipers went and cased the headquarters of the gang. In the mean time Rob, Sam, and Ollie spent the day making sure they had enough ammo. They oiled and cleaned their guns with equipment stolen from Joe's Gun Shop. And they made sure they had enough sacks to carry the cash. They decided early that everyone in the headquarters would die.

It was early evening. Clouds rolled over the mansion like steam on a counter top. Mable had just brought out some lamb with mashed potatoes and gravy. Rob started filling his plate right off. Sam gave him a disgusted look.   "What?" Rob asked with meat hanging out the side of his mouth and then they all laughed. Ollie broke off the laughter.

"We have to get ready," said Ollie. "The snipers are already in position. They report that the gang is hold up in an old school building. It was devastated by a sinkhole years ago and never reconstructed. They report half the school is accessible. Now, everyone must use their numbers so that the snipers know where you are and who you are. They might see the yellow stripe but not know who it is, Sam, you're number two; Rob you're number three. So if you say anything you first have to say, this is number two, tell them what you want,

and then ask them if they copy. Now pay attention, boys.
The snipers are Alpha, Beta, Delta, and Gamma. Their
positioning is based on where the front is. Alpha and
Beta are left and right front. Delta and Gamma left and
right rear." The boys agreed and knew what to do and
proved it by repeating it to Ollie.

"So, you have to know where you are in relation
to the front of the building. The snipers have scopes but
their vision will be limited by the building and trees." He
looked at the boys and made them repeat what he had
just told them. He felt sure they understood. Ollie
grabbed one of the maps. He said into his face mic,

"This is number one. Is the building secure?" In
his earpiece he heard,

"Lookouts are in position." The boys had just put
their earpieces and face mics on and heard the same.
Then Ollie said,

"Copy that. Team leaders in motion."

"Roger," came the reply from Alpha sniper. They
grabbed their gear and gave the sacks to one of Ollie's
men to bring to the trucks. They stowed their gear in a
black Town and Country van that only Ollie knew was
stolen. The side and back windows had been tinted limo
black. Ollie drove the twenty miles and parked
four blocks from the school. They trotted down back
alleys and kept away from the street lights.
Communication became spotty as some kind of
interference came across the airwaves. Their
communication system was running off a transmitter
that the sniper team put together. It had a thirty mile
radius, but nothing in life is perfect, is it? The
transmitter was meant to be in the field, not right next to
TV and radio broadcasts.

Ollie pulled out the map that showed the
individual buildings surrounding the area. He took the
boys halfway down a block and into a yard. The roof had

caved in on this house from a prior tornado and no one was living in it at the time. The house was across from the school. They set up shop on the first floor and began their surveillance of the school. Ollie spoke into the mic,

"Number one to Alpha. Do we have a count on the targets?" Ollie's earpiece buzzed with low feedback.

"Alpha to number one. We have six front and center and three back."

"Copy that," said Ollie. "Number one out. Okay, boys. Now we have two choices. We can observe for a while and see what happens or we can get on with the job. We can't see inside. We can't get any closer to observe where they are inside but if we take out those guys on the outside we can do the inside work ourselves." Rob said,

"Let's go inside and get it over with. All this creeping around makes me think of James Bond and that fool gets caught at least once in every film." Sam smiled at Rob and then looked over at Ollie.

"If we have what it takes to do the job tonight, then let's do it." Ollie spoke up,

"You know boys, these snipers are not going away after we get in. They won't leave their post till we are fast away. If somebody is chasing us as we leave through a door, the snipers will pick them off."

The boys told Ollie how they would do the job and since it made sense to Ollie, he had no problems with it. Rob was going in the front with Ollie and Sam was going in the back. Sam had left to get himself into position. He was the shorter of the two and he was good at shinnying around bushes and the like. So Rob and Ollie waited to hear from Sam. It wasn't five minutes when Ollie and Rob's earpieces spoke to them.

"Alpha to number one."

"Number one here." Suspense was building and blood pressures were rising.

"Visual on number two. Clear." Sam was almost in position. No one had seen him.

"Delta confirms. Package has arrived in position and is ready."

"Number two in position," Sam said. Now it was time for Rob and Ollie to make their move. The crawled out of the gangway of the house and flattened up by the side of a car. They made their way around the car and across the street. They had to go up the center of the school because it had a large courtyard where the kids had recess. The whole school was fenced in. There were bushes along the edge of the school. They made it to the bushes without being discovered. Ollie said in his mic,

"Project Open Sesame will begin in three, two, one, mark." At the word "mark," nothing happened. They heard nothing. The boys and Ollie watched the front of the building and the two guards at the front door. Sam stuck his head from the side of a bush to see what was happening. All of a sudden, one of the guards looked like his legs were knocked out from under him. The other's head shook back and forth a second and then fell straightforward down a small flight of stairs. Some static came through the earpieces.

"Alpha to one. Targets eliminated."

"Beta to one. Targets eliminated."

"Gamma to one. Targets eliminated."

"Delta to one. Targets eliminated."

Ollie stood up and took a survey of the grounds. He ran for the front door, confident in the snipers' abilities. He kept under the sills of the windows. As they approached the front doors, Ollie took the handle. He opened the door until it revealed a sliver of light and he could look in.

No one was standing inside the door. The door opened outward so he pulled out of his pocket some oil and squeezed some on the hinges. He waited a minute.

By then, the oil had done its work and Ollie opened the door enough for him and Rob to slip inside the building. There was music playing and they heard voices. There was a second set of swinging doors. Ollie pushed on them and they moved without any noise.   The hallway was standard for schools of that time. It was about ten foot wide and had a medium olive green wainscoting on the walls. Black terrazzo covered the floor and all the woodwork was stained in dark oak. A pushpin board enclosed in a glass case still hung on the wall. As Rob walked up to it. He saw one paper was still hanging by a pin. It showed there was a sixth grade play entitled King Arthur coming in January years ago. Ollie and Rob hugged the wall along the corridor.

Ollie poked his head around the corner. There wasn't anyone in the hallway. He could see the backside where the school crushed in on itself. Bricks filled half the hallway. The second classroom on the right had a light on in it. That was where the music was coming from. They worked their way down to the doorway and Rob stuck one eye around the corner. He saw one kid sitting at the teacher's desk, counting money listening to a boom box over in a corner of the room. There was no indication that others were in the room.

Rob walked through the door and right up to the kid who was fumbling for his gun. Rob's Glock made the slightest of sounds and the kid fell off the chair dead before he hit the floor. Rob didn't see the other two in the back of the room, but Ollie sprayed them with a muffled burst of his machine pistol. This room had five miniature garage doors where the kids used to hang their coats. Rob opened one up while Ollie kept watch on the entry door. Rob opened each door and exposed stacked keys of cocaine. The doors were almost six-feet in height and they were filled to the top. The desk yielded about ten thousand in cash. Rob stuck some bills in his pants.

Ollie went out to look in the hallway. There was another light down in the farthest room. It was not on before. He motioned for Rob. He almost forgot about the earpieces and mic's.

"Number one to Beta."

"Beta here."

"Can you tell me if targets are present in the room with the light on?" About ten seconds went by.

"Eyeball three at the blackboard at front of room. Motion noticed at rear of room beyond our eyes." Now Ollie had some idea where they were. They walked down to the room. Because they knew who was where, both Ollie and Rob were going to just bust in and wipe them all out. Suddenly, all kinds of racket came from downstairs. All the people in the room looked at the doorway. The earpieces crackled,

"Beta to number one, your position is compromised." Instead of Ollie and Rob rushing in, their targets were rushing out. Ollie and Rob were caught in an open area. The second the gangsters came out of the room, both Rob and Ollie pulled their triggers. They cut one guy almost in half and instantly killed the others at close range. One of them saw what happened and stayed just to the inside of the door. He was yelling at the top of his lungs how they would never get away with robbing them. The next sound that was heard was a window breaking and the thump of the gangster's body hitting the floor. The floor was due for new stain. Rob looked into the room and saw the sniper had taken care of the problem.

"Number one to Beta. Thank you," Ollie said.

Then he and Rob rushed to the stairwell. Another gunshot went off downstairs. Rob skirted the banister, almost riding it down, while Ollie covered his decent. At the landing, Rob couldn't see anything, even with half

the hallway lights beaming. He went down the last flight of stairs. Ollie moved down to Rob's old position.
Rob could hear the muttering of a machine pistol. There was a six-foot opening in the middle of the hallway. When Rob came closer he saw a sign that said lunchroom. He stuck his head around the corner and saw Sam behind the stainless steel serving counter at the far end. Blood was dripping off his shirt. He heard a shot almost right next to him. He looked around the corner and saw Sam had pinned a guy down behind a metal trashcan and table. Rob walked around the corner and using his Glock shot the guy twice. The man fell into the trashcan and then both hit the floor. Sam declared,

"There were eight of them down here and I didn't see them all. One of them stabbed me in the shoulder. I think it's pretty deep. There is a storeroom down here that is packed with cash. How did you guys do upstairs?" Rob and Ollie were walking through the lunchroom, looking at all the carnage Sam left on the floor. There was a card game going on at one table and somebody was counting cash at a table opposite the dead trash man. There were blood splatters on most of the walls. Someone had just made a Bloody Mary with an umbrella still sticking out on the top of the serving counter. Sam picked up the giant plastic martini glass and downed the drink.

For some reason, Rob felt the need to check all the pockets of the dead. It seemed Rob was changing as he was no longer affected by the death and carnage they left behind. Then he said,

"We ran into a few people, but everything is taken care of." Sam worked his way around the serving counter,

"So, Ollie, how was your first job?" Sam asked. Ollie shook his head as if to get his senses back and said,

"I wish I would have taken the lower floor." They

all laughed. Ollie spoke into his mic,

"Number one to all. Perimeter report, please."
Soft sounds of static were heard and then,

"Alpha to one. All clear."

"Beta to one clear."

"Gamma to one. We have a few neighbors who
came out when they heard the shots."

"Delta to one. Confirms neighbors. Otherwise
clear." The crew figured they would not be bothered. The
gangs that controlled this area would have a tight leash
on the people who lived around the clubhouse. They
were sure a few shots, if heard, would not arouse any
suspicions. Ollie had instructed the snipers that once
they got in if anyone showed up on the perimeter they
were to be taken out. Ollie got back on the mic,

"Number one to removal. Proceed to lower rear
doors. Okay boys, the trucks will be here in a few
minutes we need to help load them. Sam, where's the
cash?" Sam motioned with his hand to follow him. They
went through the back behind the serving station. He
took them to the school mail room. The mail room was
about twelve feet by twenty-two feet. It held little square
boxes for mail that were jammed with cash. Most were
one hundred dollar bills but one side was jammed with
twenties.

"I'll go to the doors and let them in," said Rob
happily. "and I'll grab a few sacks for each of you."
Rob returned with the sacks and three drivers. They all
started to fill the sacks with cash. This time they took
every stinking bill. The room looked empty when they
were finished. Rob went upstairs and got all the money
that was being counted in the first room they went into.
He remembered Velvet was into cocaine so he grabbed a
key of it for her and brought it back down. They filled a
truck with the cash and brought a second truck up.

"What you gonna do with that, Rob?" Ollie said pointing at the cocaine.

"This is for Velvet," Rob said.

"Whoa, boy. You don't give that much coke to an addict. She will kill herself on it. We're gonna take all the coke too. We'll distribute it in the correct amounts so she won't overdose."

"Okay, Ollie, thanks." Ollie spoke to a driver.

"Listen Joe, go upstairs and get all the crack and cocaine that's up in that room. Take a minute and look around for anything else. Don't stay too long. I'll see you at the garage." Joe nodded his understanding.   "Oh and Joe, take a key for you and your friends." Joe smiled and headed up the stairwell. "Well boys, all we need do is split out of here." Rob took a look at Sam's wound. He could see where the blade went through the jacket.

"I'll bet that hurts like hell Sam," Rob said. Sam winced a bit. They left through the back doors and walked around to the front and down to where the van was parked. Sam thought as he trotted back how simple this job was compared to the others and how nice it was to have backup snipers to take out the riff raff. It was a shame he didn't see the guy behind him, but then hindsight is twenty, twenty. He shouldn't have walked in on them all without checking how many and where they were. It was his fault. Another chalked up learning experience. Ollie said as they walked,

"We'll get back to the house and celebrate."

Chapter Fourteen

When they arrived at the precinct, Thumps helped them set up shop in the conference room. They called it a night. Cob and Dawn went and found a motel. They stopped by a local tavern to have a drink. Cob was stumped. He kept thinking about what these kids were doing. What were they trying to accomplish. So far his ideas just didn't add up. *Who kills a bunch of people and leaves all the money?* he asked himself. The ten o' clock news came on just as Dawn was ordering another tequila sunrise. Cob heard a TV reporter talk about a gang slaying. He asked the barkeep if he would turn it up.

"Chattanooga was witness to mass murder tonight when unknown assuilants entered an old school house slated for demolition next month and killed sixteen individuals. These individuals long since known as the Los Caballos gang were gunned down for no apparent reason. Speculation is that a rival gang is taking over

their territory. Their bodies, left in different rooms,
were said to be those of the highest ranking
members and even the president. The Los Caballos sent
us a statement which reads, 'We know who done this
and they will die.' That's the news...

Cob's eyes narrowed. Suddenly Cob was up out of his
chair and out the door. He to the room and opened the
door. Dawn just finished her first taste of the drink she
made.

"There's been a killing in Chattanooga. I'll bet
that's the same kids. It would confirm that they are going
south. We need to get down there. Inform the chief and
our section head. Tell him to put some people in Atlanta
and that we are going to Tennessee."

"Okay, Cob I'm on it." Dawn said. She tried to
finish her drink, but Cob stuck his head back in the door,

"You coming or what?"

"Geez, Cob. You can be a bastard," she said as she
scrambled to keep the door open in order to get through.
"Ever hold a door for a lady?" she asked. They had a six
hour drive that Cob was determined to make in four. He
was tempted to put the light on the car but regulations
wouldn't allow it. Not that he followed regulations all
that often. They stopped only once in Nashville so Dawn
could get something to eat. Cob kept telling her she was
going to get fatter than she already was. She was so
pissed she almost made him stop the car so she could
beat the hell out of him. He laughed at most of the cuss
words she used. Dawn wasn't one to start a fight, but she
could definitely finish one. They made it to Chattanooga
around five in the morning. Cob was beat from the drive.
Getting little sleep the night before didn't help matters.

"Let's get a room. I need to sleep for a few hours."
Cob suggested. Dawn went into the motel. Cob could see
the manager through the glass. He saw him hand her a

key and watched as she came back to the car.

"All they had was the Presidential suite," Dawn said with a gloomy look on her face. "It cost eighty dollars and you're paying me back." Cob scoffed at the price but said little else. He just wanted some sleep.

They walked into the room and it was huge by normal motel room standards. A small bar had tiny bottles of liquor in it. The sign on it read 'Two free bottles with rental of room. Three dollars per bottle after. Dawn told Cob that those bottles were hers for having to put up with his shit on the way here. Cob laughed. Dawn slept on the way so she wasn't tired.

"I'm going out and have some breakfast while you sleep," she said. Cob lifted his head up from where he was laying on the bed and said with a smile on his face,

"See if they can put some breakfast in a plastic container, then I will be able to have some after you drain the county of ham and eggs." Dawn shrugged that off and slammed the door. Dawn could take anything Cob dished out to her, almost. She grew up with three brothers who were a constant pain in her ass. She knew Cob was giving her shit anyway.

Dawn went into the restaurant and sat next to a couple of truck drivers. Instead of eating, she ordered a cup of coffee. The news was repeating what had happened last night. The newscaster told where the school was located. Dawn asked the driver next to her if he knew where that was. He didn't know, but his friend gave her directions. She saw the restaurant had a souvenir shop so she walked around looking at the different items. She picked something up that said 'See Ruby Falls' with a picture of water falling down from a rocky crevice. She thought to herself, I bet it looks just like the picture. If you've seen this then you've seen Ruby Falls. I just saved myself fifteen bucks she thought and she grinned.

Dawn was watching some kids that came in a few minutes ago to use the bathroom. She happened to be in a place where she could see them, but they couldn't see her. These kids were pros. One would go up to the register and ask a question, taking the line of sight away from the other kids, then one of the other kids would steal some small items and stash them in their pockets. She watched this go on for about five minutes and then moved to interfere. She grabbed the first kid who was two rows ahead of her. She went around the other row and grabbed another kid by the collar. She brought them both up to the register.

"These two have been stealing your merchandise. My name is Marshal Thorn. Did you see who the parents are that these kids belong to?" The man at the register was quite surprised.

"No, marshal. I didn't see a parent come in, but then we are pretty busy."

"I understand. Well. We'll let them stand up here facing the wall until their parents come in. Or we could get an address where they live out of them and I am off the whole day so I can wait as long as it takes." Both the kids she caught heard that and looked up at her their eyes bulging with alarm.

"We didn't do anything. Let us go or will tell our father." They both cried together. Dawn smiled when they said that.

"How bout we empty your pockets into this bag? You're going to have to give it back anyway," she said. They began to yell and scream to be let go, but Dawn stood firmly between them and escape. Finally, a lady came in the store with a worried look on her face. The man asked if she was looking for her children. She nodded yes and that's when Dawn spoke up,

"Mam, I believe these are yours?" Dawn asked. The lady came to where Dawn was holding the kids.

"Carl and Denise, what are you doing there," she said a stern look on her face. She was worried that something might have happened to them. Dawn spoke again,

"I brought them here because I caught them stealing. Empty your pockets, both of you." They emptied them and handed the items to the man at the register.

"It was Carl, mom. I was just holding stuff for him," Denise said, trying to lay the blame on her brother. The mother was upset at the children but she thanked Dawn and the man at the register. She also gave him a twenty dollar bill which he tried to refuse. She had already walked out the door, whacking Carl's back end. When they got to the car, she started on Denise.

Dawn went back to the restaurant and ordered a bacon, lettuce, and tomato sandwich. She watched a little bit of the football game that blared from a ceiling television. Green Bay was not faring well against Dallas. She thought they were playing like high school kids. She also thought the referee could use a swift kick in the ass. The ref's were throwing yellow flags on every play. "Ridiculous," she mumbled. They brought her sandwich. She took a giant bite of it just as a voice in her ear said,

"Did you leave any fingers under that bread or are you into human sushi now?" Cob said with a laugh. She wanted to retaliate for that remark but she noticed she did bite off more then she could chew this time. Cob sat down next to her.

"It's time for us to go see the school. I made arrangements to be met there by Captain Larson." She finished chewing and looked at Cob,

"How was your sleep?" She asked with half a mouthful of sandwich. In answer he crossed his fingers and said,

"Phone rang. I didn't sleep. Dawn, we're going to

catch these kids in Atlanta." She put down her drink and asked,

"And just how do you know that?" Cob smiled and said,

"They don't have any other choice." He got out of his chair and started for the door. Dawn put down her drink and left money on the table, then followed him out.

They got into the car and Cob slammed on the gas. They pulled up in front of the school building about ten minutes later. They went in through the front doors and walked down the hallway. They looked in the first room.

"Did forensics find anything?" Cob asked a local cop standing there.

"I wouldn't know, sir. They don't tell us anything until it's time for us to know," said the cop. Just then, Captain Larson came and introduced himself,

"We haven't heard anything yet. All they found were bodies and bullet casings. They did notice one thing though. The bullets used to kill the men outside were seven point sixty-two millimeters. That's military issue. They came from an M-110 SASS sniper rifle. We know this because that gun has a distinctive barrel cut." Cob stood there thinking.

"Dawn, there weren't any sniper casings at any of the other scenes, were there?" Cob asked.

"Not that I remember. What are you thinking?"

"Place a call to the chief in Indianapolis. Ask if the gun shop owner had any sniper rifles, please."

"No problem Cob, I'm on it." She pulled out her phone and punched the speed dial. She had an answer for him a minute or so later.

"Cob, they cleaned out that owner's shop and not only were there no sniper rifles, there wasn't any military ammo of any kind." She felt that Cob's

perspective on the case was taking a major turn. She saw
this before when they worked the Ghetto Blocks. She
fully expected Cob to say they were going to Atlanta
before anything even happened there. Cob was still
thinking about the current information he had been
given.

"Dawn," asked Cob. "Would you call our people
down in Atlanta and ask them to find out how many
gangs there are in that city? Also see if homicide or
narcotics knows where they are headquartered. I want to
know where they keep their money." Dawn got back on
the phone. A few minutes passed. Cob could hear Dawn
on the phone. Captain Larson was checking the bodies in
the room.

"Cob." Said dawn grabbing his attention from the
captain. "There are twenty-two gangs in Atlanta, but
there are only two big enough to have a presence and a
clubhouse. They call their headquarters clubhouses
down here. There are three drug lords from Peru,
Colombia, and Venezuela. We have their addresses as
the FBI watches them daily, hoping they make a mistake.
The FBI has been on them for the past four years. That's
all they have. Does that help you?"

"Yes, in fact, it does," said Cob. "I am thinking
that the real reasons these kids are killing is because of
two things. One: they want to rid the world of gang
scum, and two: they get off on it. I think their most
logical target is the Atlanta gangs. One of them will be on
their next list."

"That's a pretty good assumption, Cob. What I
hate about it the most is that it makes sense. But we
thought about this before. Does this mean we're going to
Atlanta?" Dawn asked. Cob thought about that for a
moment and said,

"No. We have at least a week before they strike
again. There is a trail of blood leading back out the front

doors. One of them was hit and is bleeding pretty bad. He will have to recoup for a while before the next job. Let's get all the information on paper where we can look it over and set things up. We don't want to start misusing our resources and wasting valuable time."

Chapter fifteen

The boys and Ollie arrived at the mansion. A true celebration ensued. All were in one piece except for Sam and his knife wound. The snipers sure did make a difference. Mable tended to Sam's wound. It was bleeding a little too much for her liking. She broke open a bullet and poured it on the wound after giving it a thorough cleaning. Sam winced a bit. Then, as secretly instructed, Rob grabbed Sam. He held his arms to his sides and Mable lit the gunpowder. Sam really didn't appreciate that. The cuss words he used were heard throughout the house. Even the maid came in from the back rooms. The gunpowder cauterized the wound and stopped the bleeding. Ollie, however, was in great spirits. He had never before known such excitement. They decided to lay low for a while giving Sam the time needed to heal up.

The girls, Velvet, Goldie and Sugar came over from the other wing. Mable put a special bandage on

Sam that was waterproof. Rob seemed to be falling in Love with Velvet. Tabitha was a faint memory now and Beth a one night stand. He didn't care that she was a whore living out of Ollie's wallet. Rob knew she may return to that life, but for now she was his world. They splashed in the pool together and made love in the grotto. Ollie used to boast about the grotto being a direct duplicate of Hugh Hefner's at the Playboy mansion.

Sam didn't let anyone close to him. He used women so he could get off, but he wasn't the relationship type. Sam had a secret plan. He knew that someday he would have to answer for what he has done. It was only a matter of time. No sense in getting stuck on a single girl, at least right now. If they did make it overseas and buy a place in Spain then he might get serious. Live by the bullet, die by the bullet he figured. Ollie's resources had made the fun last a little longer. He could tell Ollie was hooked on the suspense. He detected a little blood lust in the way Ollie spoke after killing a few people. It didn't pay to care because you can't bring them back and say, sorry. This was real life drama. Sam figured it was going to get worse before it got better.

It was late on a Tuesday afternoon. Ollie came into the pool house with some BBQ steaks and potatoes. It was a real feast. The boys chowed down along with the girls, except Goldie who ate nothing but salads. She said fat gave her to much energy. They had been living it up with Ollie and the boy's new found money for the last four days. They ended up with seven million dollars in cash. With fifteen million in cocaine that was being sold through Ollie's contacts in Canada.   They were living high and large. They just couldn't go out and spend it. Sam could tell Ollie was getting antsy. He wanted to go back out and have some more fun. Sam was getting a bit tired of Goldie. Goldie could give it out and take it in. Her parents were dope addicts. She spent her younger years being molested by her mother's boyfriends. Her mother wouldn't listen when she complained. One day she came across a guy who said he handled girls and if she was willing to put out, she could make the big bucks, then she could get out of the world she was living in. She took his advice and worked for him for about two years. Then Ollie shows up and bought her from the guy. That was three years ago.

Velvet was a playgirl from Moulin Rouge. She was a dancer since she was thirteen. She turned hooker because she got hooked on coke. She was still obsessed with dancing and would put on performances for the wealthy. Ollie found her and took over her contract. She performed once a week for Ollie as part of her new contract. She would enlist the help of Goldie and Sugar, but neither could dance at the caliber of Velvet. Velvet never knew her parents. The closest thing to a parent she had was Ollie.

Sugar was a southern lady. She owned a brothel for many years in Texas. She fell in love with Ollie while he was traveling and stopped by for her services. Ollie tried bull riding, and being a rodeo clown because he thought it might be exciting. He visited her brothel along with everyone else on the tour during his rodeo days. He finally convinced her to come live with him. He paid a manager to run her place. She talked with the girl who managed every week. While the other girls lived in the west wing, Sugar had the run of the house and stayed in Ollie's bed. She was older than the other girls were and so by age alone, she was the madam of Ollie's house. Nothing got past her. She controlled anyone working around the house for Ollie. The only one she did not control was Mable. Mable controlled the kitchen and inside staff. Ollie had become used to Sugar's ways. It was like having a wife without being attached by paper.

The boys were having a blast. They loved every

minute of it. Rob began to notice that Ollie was getting a bit antsy. Ollie would just lie around the pool in a leather chair and watch everyone having fun. Just two days before, he was jumping around and screwing in the grotto. Sugar did not approve of it, but didn't say anything. Sam knew the rush and excitement wears off after a while. On Wednesday morning, after they had breakfast, Sam said at the table,

"Ollie, I have been thinking. My shoulder is much better. I can move it without it hurting. I think we need to plan the next R and R mission." Rob looked at Sam his unknowing look caused him to question.

"What do you mean, R and R?" He asked. Sam laughed at Rob.

"What, do you think I was talking about rest and relaxation? I'm talking Rob and Retire. That's what this is all about." Ollie laughed. Rob just looked at Sam and said,

"Silly ass."

They brought out the maps from the safe room. Ollie dumped them on the table. They showed areas of Atlanta that would be the best. Ollie began by pointing out the differences for the boys.

"Okay, boys. Now Atlanta is controlled by drug lords, but there are gangs that have footholds in a few areas. The gangs get their blow from the drug lords. The smallest cartel is from Peru. They have a place in East Point off of Route eighty-five. It is estimated that they deal about two million a week. They gather in a clubhouse to take care of payroll debts and sales. They keep about ten people to guard the house during these times.

Then there are the Venezuelans. They control the Stone Mountain region. They have an old plantation in Redan, which is a small town southeast of Atlanta. They do about eight million a week and close up the gates of the mansion every Saturday and post guards. Now, the Colombian cartel is the biggest and the most notorious. These guys operate out in the open. They bring in nineteen million a week controlling the North and Northwest areas. They have twenty people covering their estate. Ten of them are inside security. Peace among the lords is solid because there was an agreement made many years ago by senior members. No one wants to break it."

Sam was impressed with all the information Ollie was able to gather. He had to make a choice for this job and Rob did too. He wondered what Rob was thinking,

"Okay, I say we do the Colombians." Rob threw up his hand and said,

"Me too. If this will be our last hurrah then we should go for the big bucks. Personally I can't wait to get to Europe. I've been looking at the World Residences magazine in Ollie's bathroom and it looks quite interesting." Ollie chimed in,

"Okay, then. The Colombians it is. I'll get the snipers to survey the area and fill us in before we make any moves." Just then Mable brought in dinner and they all sat down to eat. The girls came to visit and sat near their prospective evening friend. Mable served the ham and everyone began stuffing themselves. Goldie said,

"I have an idea for the back garden Ollie."

"Really!" exclaimed Ollie. "I would like to hear this idea." Goldie began to talk about the things she would change and add to the garden. She really was a flower child. She liked to receive roses from close friends. Her favorite flower was the Lilly. She didn't care which type of Lilly or what color because they all looked fantastic. She thought they would make a great addition to the garden. She had shown Ollie a map of the garden and explained where she thought the walkway should go. She believed that plants with flowers and colors must surround the human being. Ollie agreed and asked her to talk with the gardener about how fast he could get the job done for her. Ollie put her in charge of the job.

Velvet thought a theater would be nice to have also. It would require another addition to the house. Ollie said that they could tear down the tennis courts because no one played anyway. Mabel said it was becoming an eyesore. So he put Velvet in charge of that. Ollie looked at Sugar,

"Is there anything you would like to add, Sugar?" he said with a smile on his face. She thought for a second and said,

"No Hun, I think enough work is going to get done as it is. I will try and help both the girls if they wish." Ollie agreed.

"Okay, then. We had some great food, but the boys and I have some work to consider. We'll see you ladies later on." Just then his phone rang. It was the sniper crew. They were in position but they had company. Sniper Alpha told of the problem,

"Number one. We're seeing a van parked in what we would consider a strategic location to the target. We believe it is a surveillance vehicle from the FBI or other governmental agency." Ollie didn't like what he was hearing.

"Damn. How many do you think we have to deal with?" Ollie asked.

"It has been our experience that inside could be anywhere from two to six agents. Usually one monitor and two agents. Without eyes inside, it would be hard to tell."

"Thank you for the information. Set up communications and we will contact you on radio. You do know our purpose is of a higher order than a governmental agency?"

"Roger that, number one. They do have the

means to pick up our transmissions with their equipment. May I suggest we use land line for now?"

"Yes. You're right about that. Okay, I'll call you," said Ollie.

"Alpha out." Was the last thing the sniper said. Ollie looked at the boys.

"We have a problem with the target," said Ollie. "Alpha reports we have agents interested in the Colombians. They could be from any government organization. The agents are stationed in a van near the site. There may be up to six agents on-board. We're going to have to deal with them. I would prefer not to kill them."

"Who cares!" Rob said. "If they are accessible then we take them out before we go in." Sam gave his friend a startled look. This wasn't the Rob he started out with.

"What if they have communication to the outside? The place could be swarming with more agents than Carter has liver pills. In half the time it takes to swallow them too," said Sam. Ollie jumped in,

"He's right, Rob," Ollie said with a serious look on his face. "We're going to have to think about this and make a plan. If we go in there all gangbusters, we might end up on the wrong end of the gun. I also wonder, if the feds are watching the Colombians, the Colombians might be watching too. So, if we take out the watchers, we may be found out ourselves and be unable to close on our job. I just thought of something. I'll be back in a minute." Ollie left the room. The boys watched him walk down the hall and into a doorway on the right. Rob turned to Sam and said,

"I don't see what the problem is. We riddle the van full of bullets and move onto our target." Sam gave Rob a disgusted look as if he didn't hear anything he or Ollie were saying.

"Look, Rob. If we do it that way as long as you understand we may expose ourselves to the drug lord. And then he will have an army out front protecting his estate. He can also call in reinforcements from the gangs who sell the coke for him. Then we're screwed." Ollie came back from down the hall holding a canister with a hose attached.

"Boys. This is sleeping gas," Ollie said excited. "I got it from a dentist going out of business who owed me some money. I bought his place and resold all the instruments, equipment, and then the building. Made a little profit too, but this stuff I couldn't sell. There was something about inspecting it and a seal and God knows what. If we can get this into the front of the van the agents will be fast asleep, any ideas?"

Sam thought for a second.

"They probably don't lock their front doors in the vans do they? I mean, who is going to fuck with an FBI van? I can sneak up, open the door, hold my breath, turn on the canister and shut the door. What do you think?" Rob nodded approval. Ollie thought it might be a little risky. What choice did they have?

"I'm okay if you're going to promise to be careful." They all put their headgear on. Everything was in working order and it was starting to get darker outside. Clouds blew in from the west shutting out the moon. Ollie called from his cell to Alpha.

"Alpha here."

"Report on conditions, please."

"All is quiet. Van still in position. No activity. Sentries posted outside of target. We have brought a fifth for backup. She will run video loop inside the camera system. Switch to channel thirty-seven. The channel is far enough away so it won't bleed."

"Roger, Alpha. Team leaders in motion."

"Acknowledged," answered the sniper.

Chapter Sixteen

Cob and Dawn walked into the precinct conference room and began to look over the maps. Dawn headed for the coffee machine and swiped a doughnut out of the box on the counter. She moved closer to Cob and bit into it. Icing sprinkled onto the map. Cob looked up at her, turned, and walked out of the door. He came back a few seconds later with his own doughnut. He began munching happily. Cob was in between bites when Dawn said quietly,

"I agree with what you said about Atlanta. The way these kids are moving from state to state. Makes me believe there's a sort of sense to it all. I'm starting to feel they are getting information from somewhere." An officer walked in the room cutting off Cob's response.

"Someone to see you, sir. Mr. Montgomery from Indianapolis. He's a private investigator." The officer just stood there waiting. He was right out of the academy and not quite used to thinking like a cop yet.

"Are you going to show him in?" Cob demanded grimly. "Or would you like me to go fetch him myself?"

"Oh, no sir, I'll be right back." The officer said.

Cob turned back to Dawn.

"Yes, I see your point. You're saying there is a possibility they are getting help somehow, friends maybe." Cob posited. The officer returned with Mr. Montgomery in tow. Cob offered his hand.

"Good morning sir, how can I help you?" Cob asked. Mr. Montgomery shook Cob's hand and then let go.

"Marshal, I did something concerning the two kids you're after. I feel real bad about it." Cob looked at him and was instantly interested.

"You mean you talked with them? Please tell me what you talked about." Montgomery took a seat next to the conference table.

"The boys contacted a mutual acquaintance of mine wanting to hire my services. I usually do divorce information, spying, cheaters, family heirs and missing persons. I met with the two kids. They wanted to hire me to find out where all the drug cartels and gang headquarters were located. I was skeptical about their motives for wanting the info so I questioned them. The one called Sam seemed to be the one in charge. He said that his sister was abducted by a member of one of the gangs. They needed to find her and bring her back home. Apparently she was in love with one of gangbangers. It made sense at the time. Naturally I felt sorry for the kids so I got a hold of some friends of mine and got the information. When I saw the carnage they left behind I first thought it was to get their sister out. I knew something was going on when all the rival gangs started going after each other." Cob was giving him his undivided attention.

"Tell me about the one called Sam. What was he like?" Cob asked.

"Well. He seemed calculating, smart, perhaps above average intelligence. He said all the right things to get me to provide the info they needed."

"Did you meet or talk to the other kid?"

"I didn't talk to him. He sat next to Sam and watched every move I made. I got the picture Sam was the leader."

"Did they say anything else like where they were going or."

"Nope. Just that they wanted his sister back."

Cob sat for a moment and thought about what he just heard.

"This changes some things we had been thinking about. Thank you, Mr. Montgomery. You have been a great help. The officer will see you out. Thanks again. Dawn?" Dawn came into the room with another doughnut. Cob smiled.

"We're going to Atlanta and we're leaving now. I want to get there before dark. Get with the FBI and find out who are the more active of the cartels. See if we can get hooked up by video or sound with their people in the field. I assume they are monitoring the cartels down here like they do in Chicago."

"Okay Cob, I'm on it," Dawn said. She hastily put down her doughnut and slipped the phone out of her pocket. They walked quickly out of the room and down the hall to the parking lot. Cob was talking to Captain Larson and thanking him for everything. They got into the car and Cob slammed on the gas.

"We're headed off to round them up," Cob said more to himself and the car than to Dawn. They had a two and a half hour drive to Atlanta where it had been raining. It was rush hour, and as always, traffic tended to be slow and aggravating. It was a typical fall day with overcast sky. Humidity made you feel stuffed up and older people who shouldn't have a license brought the slow lane into its reality. They made the trip in two hours. Cob had a lead foot when it called for it.

Atlanta's marshal unit had a van, but Cob didn't know if it was deployed or whom it was watching. The FBI agreed to allow them access to existing units. They were ten minutes from any one of them. According to the attending agents, everything was quiet, a normal day so far they said. Their driver was filled in on the locations. Cob and Dawn were given seats in front of screens. They couldn't see anything, but they could hear the general conversations. The conversation they heard consisted of the agents' lives outside of the bureau mostly. Some agents' told jokes about their fellow agent's indiscretions or failed exams. All parties knew they were keeping an eye on each of the cartels.

The van that Cob and Dawn were in did not have the advantage of knowing which cartel the guys were talking about. They were just tuned into the FBI frequency. At times there was confusion as to what was happening and where. The problem was little was happening. Their van was on loan from the FBI. Cob was frustrated since they could not see anything. They heard yelling and chairs falling and then nothing.

"What the hell was that?" Cob asked. "Where did it come from?" He demanded with a certain alarm in his voice.

"We don't know. Let's wait to see if there is more," said one of the operators. He tried to get the receiver settings in place. "This type of thing happens when they see a runner that is wanted by Interpol. They usually jump out of the vehicle to make an apprehension. They might gain access to the cartel's main house using 'harboring a fugitive' as reason for entry and probable cause."

About ten minutes passed before somebody decided to call one of the agents on their cell and got no answer. Cob started to yell at the driver to get the van started. He asked Dawn to call the other agents and she reported they were okay at Peru and Venezuela. That meant the commotion came from Colombia. Cob yelled at the driver,

"Get us to the Colombian estate, now!" The driver yelled back,

"Hold on! We're going for a ride," and promptly smashed his foot into the gas pedal. The van lurched forward. Two agents and the marshals were thrown into the back doors. The van's tires screeching on the asphalt.

Chapter Seventeen

The boys and Ollie hopped into the limo and the driver punched the gas. They had some time to waste so Sam began reading a magazine and Rob turned on the TV and found some cartoons. The boys were both sitting on the limo's side seat. Ollie had the back seat all alone and had the maps out. He was transferring them to a smaller page he could keep in his jacket. This job wasn't going to be a hard. It just required fine tuning. Specific things had to happen at certain times. He knew the snipers would perform. He just hoped the rest of them could.

Ollie was getting bored. the new strategy didn't keep him occupied enough. He ran through the stages once again in his head. He thought maybe there was something wrong with him, brain tumor or something. Who could have it all and not give a shit about any of it? He thought after this job he would lock the house up and travel into the mountains. Maybe he would start a moonshine still and if the girls didn't want to come then the hell with them. Even with his old friend, Ollie was a lonely man, in a lonely time. He thought about paying every cent he had for a trip to the Space Station. He also thought about building a glass submarine to seek the oceans depths. He wanted to do something that he had not been done before. Then it occurred to Ollie that what he was doing now with the boys was something no one else had done.

The car pulled into the designated warehouse rented for the occasion. The boys started putting on the rest of their gear while Ollie got the maps together. Ollie put on his head gear,

"Number one to Alpha. Situation report."

"Alpha to one. No van activity since last report. Target guards dispersed. Team members report.

"Beta ready."

"Gamma ready. Guards unloading panel truck."

"Delta ready. Guards at entryway."

"Sigma ready. Overhead from pole position. Ready to cut TV loop and install dead screen."

"Roger that. Team leaders in motion," answered Ollie. They walked a brisk pace for one block to the residence. They threw hooks over a long-limbed oak and climbed a makeshift net. Ollie prepared the gear a little different this time. He had his yard man cut up three pieces of steel that fit inside the backpacks they all carried. They made one to cover their chests also. Having the steel gave them at least some protection along with the bulletproof vest they wore. Rob complained of the weight, but Sam told him he would be wearing it for about ten to twenty minutes.

Ollie paid the sniper crew double what they got last time just to make sure there were no problems. All the trucks were in place back at the warehouse. Their engines running on full tanks of gas. Rob and Ollie went over the wall and got into position. Sam had the canister in his backpack and worked his way across the street. The surveillance van was parked on his side of the street.

Sam came out at the back side of the van where no one could see from the inside. So far the plan was working. There were six foot high hedges surrounding the side of a house where the van was located. The agents put the van there so the people in the house would not wonder why it sat in the same place all day.

Sam moved through the bushes in a crouched position. He quietly stepped to the side of the van. He glanced inside. There was no one in front. He pulled on the door handle and found it was unlocked. It didn't make a noise opening. He took a deep breath and flung the door open. He turned the valve of the canister on and positioned the hose toward the back of the van. He then dropped the canister on the front seat and closed the door. He went to the back of the van and put his body up against the doors. There was commotion in the back of the van. Chairs spilled their contents on the floor. Voices yelling what the hell was going on and then silence. Sam went back through the bushes. He clicked his mic,

"Operation sandman complete. Will rendezvous in four minutes." Sam almost ran across the front yards to the side of the wall where Rob and Ollie went over. He climbed the net and pulled it up over the wall with him. He found Rob and Ollie. Ollie patted Sam on the back and clicked his mic,

"Number one to Alpha. Team leaders in place, commence drop shipment."

"Acknowledged," was Alpha's reply. The boys and Ollie took binoculars from their packs and focused on the guards in the front. Their attention was cut short by static in their earpiece. Then,

"Alpha to mobile team. Commence drop shipment." Just as Alpha said those words, a man at the front of the house jerked his head to the side. His arms went soft like rubber. A second later he fell face first to the ground. Sam figured the guy didn't feel a thing. The two guards at the back of the house turned when they heard the other guy drop. A bullet slapped one in the shoulder and went through his neck. The same bullet ripped through the eye of the other guard. It bounced around in his skull and came out just below the ear on the other side. They both fell onto each other like lovers to the stairs below.

A shot came from the top of the house. A widow walk went around the center of the roof. Widow walks were popular back in the day. Wives would walk around on them while waiting for their captain husbands to return. A second later the man was slumped over the railing. Three bullets hit the man on the widow walk at once. He seemed to do a jerky dance before he went waist high over the railing. His gun sliding down the roof shingles landing muzzle first in the grass. Rob had another guy's face in his binoculars as he came to the front looking for who was shooting his friends. His face turned toward Rob just as a hole appeared right between his eyes. His head jerked back and then snapped forward. His lifeless eyes glazed over in death.

"Alpha to number one. Drop shipment is compete."

"Acknowledged," said Ollie. Ollie and the boys walked hunched down over to the back side of the house. The snipers couldn't see the cartel unloading the vans. They peaked around a corner. A cartel member smoking a cigarette came into view near the back door. Rob took out his Glock. He came around the corner surprising him. The cartel member recognized Rob was not one of his crew. Rob's Glock made a muffled snort like someone shaking out a towel from a washer. The cartel member's legs crumbled underneath him as he fell to the ground. Rob and Ollie went to the door an opened it just a sliver. Ollie went in first.

There were two cartel members positioning boxes filled with cash and three guys playing cards in the back. Ollie didn't waste any time. He sprayed the room and bodies were thrown out of chairs and on top of boxes. One died head down on the table with a cigar still between his teeth. Nice quick way to go thought Ollie. Ollie called the trucks in motion and had Sigma open the gate. Then was gone around the corner.

Ollie opened the door to the garage and was met by a stream of hot lead that knocked him back from the door. His steel plate taking the brunt of the bullets came loose during the first impact. Not all the bullets missed their mark. He fell to the ground. His leg jammed in the doorway. Delta took advantage of the opening to send the three inside on their way to the pearly gates for judgement.

When he fell back his leg jammed the door open giving Delta a clear view into the garage. Within a span of seconds the three inside the garage were on their way to the pearly gates.

"Delta to number two and three. Number one is down in front of garage. Positioning to plan B." Escape plan B was drastic. Ollie set it up as a contingency plan in case any of the three of them were hurt. It meant they were neither compromised nor over run but getting out was the course of action. For Ollie, who read sci-fi books, it was better to live to fight another day than to die a martyr. Ollie couldn't speak from the fits of coughing. Blood soaked his shirt. Sam knew the plan meant the snipers would watch their backs while they escaped. Sam and Rob ran to the garage and popped two guys who had just arrived. They saw the bodies and they saw Ollie. They picked him up shoulder to shoulder.

"How bad is it, Ollie? Sam asked. Ollie coughed some more.

"Not bad, kid. The bullet went in and out. I'll be

alright. It's part of the experience," Ollie said with a gasp. They dragged Ollie to the edge of the grass and watched the trucks make it through the front gate. Sirens could be heard in the distance. They were getting louder. The boys drag walked Ollie toward the wall where they came in. Sam said,

"The cops are on the way here. We have to get out of here now." Rob nodded agreement and continued to drag Ollie's body. Ollie could barely walk. They got to the wall just as the police entered the driveway. They were like rats swarming through the grounds. They caught all the drivers and slammed them up against the trucks.

Cob and Dawn with their guns drawn walked alongside the mansion. Local cops spread out alongside them. They took cover behind a bush or giant potted plant base.

"We want them alive, people!" Cob shouted to the masses. Cob stopped at the end of the building. A few cops walked past to get a look at the area crouching down low. Suddenly one of the cops was pushed from the top of his head onto his back. Cob looked and half the side of the man's head was missing.

"Hold up, everyone. There's a sniper out there. Take cover," he yelled. Cob thought the kids might be trapped inside. Everyone stopped dead in their tracks. Cob put an arm in front of Dawn who was trying to peak around the corner. He gently pushed her back to the wall behind him.

Rob and Sam heaved Ollie's body over the wall. Ollie couldn't stop coughing up blood. The police had surrounded the house. They were coming toward where the boys were hiding. Two cop cars closed off the street. The cops were out holding back bystanders while others had their guns at the ready. They went from bush to bush checking the perimeter.

"Ollie," said Sam, "you have to get up and try and

move. We have to make it to the next street so we can steal a car." Ollie's eyes showed he had little strength, but he made the attempt to get up and walk. The boys lifted the majority of his weight for him. They walked and hopped a bit and made it past the cops who were looking on their side of the street. Suddenly, a car came down the alley right in front of them. Sam took out his Glock and moved to the door. It was a woman. She saw the gun started to scream. Sam shot though the window, opened the door, and pulled her bloody carcass out of the car. Her purse and groceries fell out also. The boys placed Ollie's body in the back with Rob. Sam punched the gas pedal and headed for the highway.

Cob and Dawn, now uncertain whether to move or not, made an effort to round the corner one at a time. Cob went first. Cob made it and went inside the house. Dawn followed. A minute later three officers walked around the other corner. *The snipers must be gone,* thought Cob.

Once inside they saw the carnage left by Ollie and Rob. It looked like something picked them up and threw them around the room. They formed a team and checked every room in the house. The FBI came in and announced that high-ranking members of the cartel died there that day. The cops sent the drivers to jail in a paddy wagon. None of them were talking. A few minutes later a cop called in that they found a woman in the street near an alley. She was shot once in the head. Her purse and groceries were laying in the street. Cob went in the direction of the lights by the wall. The cops showed him the net used to climb the wall. He climbed the net and went over the wall. He walked across the street to where the woman was. They had a head start and Cob was not happy. He looked at the cop next to him.

"I need a car now!" The cop responded by

handing Cob the keys to his cruiser. Cob ran for it. He
damn near shoved the pedal through the floor in his
haste to get out of the hood. He drove toward highway
seventy-five. He got on the phone calling Dawn to find
the woman's drivers license and to see what kind of car
she owned.

Rob was pressing on Ollie's wound trying to stop
the bleeding. It wasn't coming out fast. Ollie's coughing
had increased. Sam went down the ramp to highway
seventy-five North. He kept the car at the speed limit so
he wouldn't attract attention. Cob was driving up
highway seventy-five with the phone against his ear.

"What kind of car am I looking for, Dawn?" He
yelled into the phone.

"It's a Ford Galaxy five hundred. It's an older
model with large engine. Lots of horses, Cob. The plates
are Alpha Bravo two nine John X-Ray," she repeated the
plate for him. Cob was flying north on seventy-five and it
never occurred to him that he might be going the wrong
way. He was traveling through Kennesaw when he
spotted a gray Galaxy in the fast lane. Traffic was
horrible because everyone who went to the ballgame
were on their way home. He moved to the middle lane
and got a better look at the driver. It was Sam. He was
paying attention to the road. Cob turned on the cruiser
lights and said into the loud speaker,

"Pull over to the side of the road." Sam turned to
look at the cop car. He stepped on the gas and the Galaxy
moved well out in front of the cruiser. Just as Cob moved
to get behind them and try a pit maneuver, Sam shot
across three lanes of traffic. He went up a ramp and
scared the hell out of a bunch of people. Sam moved the
car down to highway forty-one and punched it. He was
almost in Dalton now and not far from Ollie's home. He
would try to lose this guy in the backwoods.

Cob lost him by the time he reached the end of the ramp. *If I were him,* Cob Thought, *I'd still be trying to go north.* Cob headed for highway forty-one. Once on the four lane road he started to search for the car again. He found Sam just outside of East Ridge heading into Chattanooga. Cob swerved over two lanes cutting off a trucker. He fired at Sam's tires. The shot knocked the hub cap off the back wheel. Then he took a shot at Sam since he was in the far lane with no traffic on his other side. The shot broke out the side window and surprised Sam who thought he had lost him. Sam stepped on the gas and the Galaxy moved ahead. Cob brought his cruiser into position behind the Galaxy. Sam was no fool. He slammed on the gas and swerved over to a turning lane and shot off on State Road twenty-seven.

Cob followed. He caught the back end of a vehicle with his bumper and spun it around. The car slid sideways off the road. Cob was chasing Sam down twenty-seven. Suddenly Sam took a sharp turn. There was no way for Cob to imitate the turn without tiping the cruiser. He slammed on the breaks and jammed the vehicle in reverse back to where Sam had cut off road. Sam was at least a few blocks ahead. They were smack in the middle of an old country road not even on the map. Cob lost site of the car. He kept driving down the road but slowly so he wouldn't be ambushed. He came to an opening where a huge mansion stood out of nowhere. Cob hit the breaks in front of it, popped out of the car, and stood aiming over the door. He saw the car and there was movement.

"Hold it right there, it's all over," yelled Cob. "You have no place to go. You'll be surrounded in ten minutes."

Sam started dragging Ollie's body. Rob answered Cob's statement with some fire power. The bullets ripped off Cob's side view mirror and pushed Cob to the ground to avoid being snagged by hot lead. When he got up they were inside the house. Nothing he could do now but bring in some backup. Cob wondered why when he tried to use the radio he wasn't getting an answer. He found that he had somehow ripped out the microphone cord during the chase. Dawn pulled up a few minutes later.

"How did you know where to find me?" Cob asked.

"The cruisers down here have Lojack on them. We've been following you. It seemed like every time we set up a roadblock or spikes on the highway, the kid would drag you somewhere else. We tried to compensate but it wasn't getting us anywhere. We just decided to follow you. We would storm the surrounding area whenever you stopped."

"It's a good thing you did," Cob said with a look of relief on his face. "The kids are holed up in the house. It looks like they have a casualty. Older man about thirty or so I would say. Let's find out who owns this house."

Rob helped Sam take Ollie to his bed but Ollie wouldn't have it. He was coughing up blood now more than ever. He kept saying

"Safe, safe." Sam kept telling him that they were in his house and safe for the moment. There were at least a dozen cars out front now. Rob said,

"What the hell are we going to do now?" His question seemed to reverberate in their ears.

"I don't know Rob, let me think," said Sam. Then they heard some broken glass and a tear gas grenade went off in the living room and two other rooms. A swat team made one hell of a racket as they came in through the roof windows. The boys readied their guns, but Ollie grabbed Sam's arm and pulled him down.

"Take me to the shelter." All the girls showed up crying. Then Sam knew what to do. He called the girls over. He asked them to help Rob drag Ollie's body to the shelter and lift him up putting his face close to the speaker. Ollie said, "Molly Hatchet." The safe door opened. Everyone went inside, Sam hit the emergency shut button he saw earlier, and the door swung closed. Rob said,

"Well that's just great. Now we're cooped up in here for ten years." Sam looked at Rob.

"Would you rather be outside coughing and crying while they fill your body full of holes?" Rob laughed. Sam went to check on Ollie. The girls put him in a bed. Ollie motioned for Sam to come over. He said to Sam,

"Sam, behind the mirror in the hallway are two things. One thing is cameras so you can see everything that is going on outside." A fit of coughing took Ollie. ?If you turn the medallion star a door will open and a mile long tunnel will lead to a garage at the bottom of the mountain. Make sure you close the mirror after you enter. There is a large motor coach and Sugar knows how to drive it. It has a tiny car in the back also. Take that when you are ready to leave. Don't let these guys get you, Sammy. And with that last sentence Ollie gushed blood over his chin and passed away. Sam was crying. Sugar was crying too. She said that after checking his wound she knew it had punctured a lung and God knows what else. She didn't know how he hung on so long.

Sam asked,

"What are we going to do now?
Sugar got up and said,

"I'll show you, hun. Common girls. Sugar led them to a wall with stripes. Pressing the right place produced a door. They walked in and it was a room full of guns. The room also had rocket launchers.

"These launchers," Sugar said vengeance in her voice. "will fire through holes in the concrete. We can blow up everything outside the house. The holes are set so that anything fired up them will land in certain places. They carried the launchers to a section of the room and placed them on a stage. At first, the stage looked as though it had lights, but those were holes to the outside. They raised the stage by pressing a button. Holes opened up in the ceiling as the stage rose. Some water came in but not much. Sugar loaded a launcher and adjusted it to make sure the rocket would go up the hole. Then she pressed a button and wham! A minute later, one of the police cars blew all to hell and cops staggered back farther away. Three dead cops lay in the dirt near the burning wreck.

Cob knew something was wrong when the car blew up. He suggested storing the place. When no one agreed, he did it himself. He fired six shots at the house and broke all the glass in the foyer. He ran in only to find the swat team coming out. Cob said,

"What's up?" to the commander of the swat team.

"They've holed up inside a bomb shelter. We expect with the amount of money this guy had and their rations they might last three years in there. You want to wait for them?" Cob put his gun arm down and shuffled some glass around on the floor with his shoe. The swat commander continued,

"We have a computer man trying to break the code and open the door. It's pretty sophisticated. We don't know how long it will take." Sam, Rob and the girls were sitting on chairs in the main room.

"You want to go blow up more of those cars?" Sugar said giving the boys a hopeful look.

"No. It's not like we're going out the front door anyway," answered Sam. They all didn't seem to be worried about the cops getting in the bunker. They could nuke the place and still not succeed. Velvet and Goldie went to make sandwiches and get some drinks. Sugar offered the idea that they stay here for a while and recoup their energy. Then they could leave through the tunnel. Sam and Rob agreed. So they partied like it was 1969. They turned on some music and drank a few beers. The girls all got naked and went into the hot tub. Ollie had many game tables put in and Rob and Sam were later found at the Foosball game. Everything in the world was right for the moment.

Cob didn't know what to think. Never before had he come across a criminal mind that had all the bases covered. He thought, *was he supposed to wait three years to catch his perps.*

"Is anyone trying to cut the power to this place?" He asked to anyone.

"We cut the power to the whole grid here ten minutes ago," the swat commander said. "But there is still power to the safe door. We don't know where it is coming from. The prints used to build it have gone missing from the city inspectors department. There are four hundred homes without power right now. By all rights, this place should not have any power. The waterfall in the pool is still working. This guy was a genius."

The military came the next day and tried to shoot a rocket at the wall. It only made a twelve inch hole about one inch deep. No real damage was done to the house. The troops estimated that the walls were at least six to ten feet deep top and bottom. They tried digging on the third day. They set off enough explosives to knock down the Empire State Building. They didn't even make a dent.

It was party time for Rob and Sam. They felt the attempts to break in by those outside. One of Ollie's tree cams caught the army core of engineers digging up the ground. They stuck explosives under the house. The cable was still hooked up so they had TV and caviar and of course the girls. They played strip poker on

Thursday. It wasn't a fair game since the girls
weren't dressed anyway. Rob had to walk around with
pencils in his ears for three days because he lost and
wasn't wearing any clothes. Goldie gave everyone a good
massage and put those heat rocks on their backs. Then
everyone gave her the best massage ever. Sugar made a
rack of lamb one night and Rob said,

"Whatever happened to Mable?" The girls all
bowed their heads. Velvet answered,

"Just before we walked out to where you boys
were the Swat teams were coming in the side entry to the
pool. Mable opened the door a little too quick and scared
a cop who shot her point blank. That's when we ran to
you. We made it to you because we know the house. To a
newcomer it would appear like a maze."

"I'm sorry to hear that girls," said Rob, "she was a
great cook. No offense Sugar." Sugar had a smile on her
face.

"She was not only a good cook, she was Ollie's
body guard. She was a tenth degree black belt. A fourth
degree in Judo. A marksman, and if it wasn't for her, you
wouldn't have had the snipers." Suddenly they all heard
a sound by the safe door. It was a loud humming coming
from the other side.

Cob pulled up in the driveway. It had been three
weeks now and they were no better off than day one. He
announced to the world,

"Is anyone going to do anything to get inside this
thing?" One of the swat members came over and said,

"Yeah, we're starting to drill a hole in the door.
We can only go an inch before the bit burns up and we
have to change it, but they brought about a hundred bits.
Torches don't have enough heat to melt this steel
whatever it is." Cob looked at him like he was nuts.

"And what will you do once you break through in
a week or so?" Cob asked.

"Well. We think we can make it pretty hard on them. We can put a bunch of different gasses in there, maybe send a small rocket through or listen to their demands if we can convince them we will get in eventually. The thing is, we won't know until we get through. Then we can send in a camera lens."

"At least that is something I guess," said Cob. Cob had a hard time dealing with this situation. He always got the criminal he was after. He actually did get the criminal this time. At least they weren't going anywhere. He wanted to get behind the scenes with these kids and find out the reason they did it all. He had a feeling he wasn't going to getting any answers.

News people had been camped down the road from the house the whole time. The capture of Sam and Rob was being billed as the Siege of Chattanooga.   The authorities were stumped why they couldn't get in. They thought about posting guards and letting them stay until they ran out of food. The Mayor of Chattanooga answered a TV reporter,

"When you think about it they are just as shut up as if in jail. Granted, we do not know what kind of life they are living in there, but we are sure that it is better than being behind bars. Whatever they are doing in there, we will make it worse once the hole is drilled through."

Beyond the reporters there were two other groups. The cops had to contend with them also. One group rallied for leaving them alone. They felt they did justice to bad people and accomplished what the police had not been able to in decades. The other group wanted them all to take a seat in the electric chair.

Tabitha was getting upset each day the boys had not returned. She wondered what they were doing. She was only supposed to be there for three days. Her cell phone rang,

"Yes, I'm Tabitha Johnson..." the phone fell from her hand and she fell back on the couch. Just then her aunt Bess came in,

"Well, what on earth is the matter child?" She asked. Then the house phone rang and aunt Bess picked up the receiver,

"Hello. Yes. Oh my, when did this happen? Gangsters, you say. My lord." It was clear aunt Bess had no idea what kind of work Tabitha's daddy had gotten himself into. She went back into the living room and sat down grabbing a hold of Tabitha,

"I'm so sorry, baby. We have to keep it together, honey. We need to pack and go on down there." Tabitha got sick and wouldn't eat. She became bed ridden and solemn. She would say death was coming to get her. After two days of sulking and aunt Bess telling her they had to go down to Florida, Tabitha got out of bed. She grew angry and unhappy at the loss of her father. Aunt Bess came to her room and said,

"Pack your things, child. We're leaving in an hour." Tab knew her aunt was just trying to resolve issues with the burial, house, and the things inside it. So they left for Tampa.

They arrived in Tampa the next day. Her aunt began taking care of things . Tabitha went to see her friends. She found Marcie at the corner store. They hugged each other.

"Marcie," Tabitha said, "you have to tell me what happened." Marcie got control of herself.

"Okay Tab, this is what I saw. I was in the kitchen with Nana helping her bake a cake when these guys came in and demanded to see your father. He was downstairs so Nana said she would get him for them, but they wouldn't let her. They all went downstairs. I followed them. They caught your father coming out of a secret door and tied him to a chair. They questioned him about who he sent to do the job.

They wanted to know what happened to them after they completed the job. Your father said he didn't know. They told him it was all over the TV. They shot him in the head when he didn't tell them anything. I ran upstairs and told Nana and we both got the hell out of there. From Nana's friend's house across the street we saw them load up whatever your dad had down in the basement. Then they left. That's how it went down."

Tabitha was angry now. It was Rob and Sam's fault that her father was killed. Her eyes reddened and all she could think about was revenge. Tabitha got a call from Marcie about a day or so later.

"Tab, have you seen the news?" She asked. "They have them trapped in a house in Chattanooga. They're in some kind of shelter and the cops can't get in." Tab thanked Marcie for the information and hung up the phone.

Tabitha waited until midnight. She took the keys for the rental car and headed for Chattanooga. It took her almost eleven hours to get there and she was tired. She called the local police and asked who the man in charge of the siege was where the two boys were being held. The man on the phone told her it was a man named Marshal Barrington. She told the man where she would be at noon. She told him what she was wearing and that she had info that could help him catch the killers. Cob arrived at the diner five minutes late. He sat down on the other side of the booth. Tabitha began, red eyes almost ready to cry.

"Mr. Barrington, Sam is my cousin. The house they are in belongs to my other cousin, Ollie. He built a safe room that is I think six feet thick of special concrete. You won't be able to get in. About a mile south of the house is an old construction road and in the side of a hill is a large metal garage door. Inside is a motor coach if they haven't already used it to get away."

"Why are you telling me all this, Tabitha?" Cob asked.

"Because without knowing it, Sam and Rob killed my father. They don't deserve to live." She said with an angry look on her face.

After two weeks of drilling they finally got through. They heard loud music and saw bodies dancing quickly past the hole. The swat commander thought it was so loud in there that they didn't even hear the bit break through. They probably didn't see it either. Cob told swat to get some tear gas in there.   Swat did as they were ordered. In the mean time, Cob went down to the garage where the motor coach was located.
They would try to make their escape from here. He was sure of it. The information he got from Tabitha turned out to be true. All she wanted in return was to see them captured and thrown in jail.

Cob put her in the back seat of his cruiser and told her to stay. It was borrowed, it was clean and it was bulletproof. She had a good view of the garage. The road leaving the garage was lined with officers. All the cops had weapons of their choice, shotguns, machine guns, handguns of all kinds. They hid just off to the side under cover. If the vehicle did not stop for Cob, they were instructed to shoot to kill.   They didn't have to wait an hour. Just as the sun began to dip itself into the horizon, the great garage door opened, and out came the motor coach. There was a lady driving the vehicle. Cob stood right in front and yelled,

"Give up, you're surrounded. There is no place to go. If you do not get out of the vehicle, we will shoot to kill." Sugar lifted both her hands giving them all a finger on each hand. Then she screamed

"Fuck you all!" and slammed on the gas pedal. The motor coach leaped forward and picked up speed real fast. Cob jumped out of the way. Every officer began to unload hot lead into the coach. Sam and Rob opened a window on either side and blasted everything that moved. They took half the arsenal from Ollie's safe room in the coach.

Goldie and Velvet kicked out what was left of the back window. They started shooting rockets and sprayed the area with machine pistols, pointing at anything that moved. Sam killed three officers before he saw two aiming at Rob so he dove in front of Rob and took six bullets in the chest. Rob took two slugs in the belly. Goldie and velvet were hit by close range shot gun blasts as officers ran across the back of the vehicle.

One blast tore Goldie's arm off and the other the side of Velvets head. The impact of the shot was so forceful, it blew Goldie along a back wall and halfway through a side window. Her life force leached down the side of the coach. Sugar was killed instantly when a sniper bullet hit her just above the left eye. Her foot jammed on the pedal and kept the vehicle moving until it ran into a tree. The police rushed the vehicle cautiously and called down the ambulance. The paramedics were taking Rob out of the coach and Tabitha was there. The EMT's said he wasn't going to live much longer. She looked him right in the eye.

"Did you think I would let you get away with my father's death?" Her question hung in the air. Rob looked at her. Those deep blue eyes like pools of Caribbean water and her hair like that of an angel. He wanted to kiss her just one more time. He tried to speak, but only coughed up blood. He turned his head to the side and said, "I love you," as his face took on a somber stillness like a toy that has been switched off or a doll when its cord has run to the end of its line.

About the Author

D. Jay Thompson is an accomplished person in the home building trades. He holds an English Degree from the University of Florida and a Masters Degree in Adult Education from the University of South Florida. He currently resides in Florida with his wife and dog Bonita. His interests are many and include writing, art, music, and home remodeling. He enjoys walks on the beach.

Mr. Thompson has written the sequel to Robbin' the Hood. The adventure continues. Look for it in January 2017.

Books coming in late 2019- 20 are:

Under Shorts: Short stories under a readers scrutiny.

Singularities: A book of poems.